Beyond Recall

Mary Meigs, self-portrait.

Beyond Recall

MARY MEIGS

EDITED BY LISE WEIL

Talonbooks

Vancouver

Talonbooks
P.O. Box 2076, Vancouver, British Columbia, Canada V6B 3S3
www.talonbooks.com

Typeset in Scala and printed and bound in Canada.

First Printing: 2005

LIBRARY AND ARCHIVES CANADA CATALOGUING IN PUBLICATION

Meigs, Mary, 1917–2002.
    Beyond recall / Mary Meigs ; edited by Lise Weil.

ISBN 0-88922-505-2

    1. Meigs, Mary, 1917-2002. 2. Painters—Canada—Biography. 3. Authors, Canadian (English)—20th century—Biography. I. Weil, Lise II. Title.

PS8576.E386Z462 2005   759.11   C2004-906442-8

The publisher gratefully acknowledges the financial support of the Canada Council for the Arts; the Government of Canada through the Book Publishing Industry Development Program; and the Province of British Columbia through the British Columbia Arts Council for our publishing activities.

CONTENTS

EDITOR'S INTRODUCTION

When Verena Stefan and I first proposed to Mary the idea of a book of her writings about old age, she seemed doubtful. Ever since the stroke in August of 1999 her faculties had been steadily dimming—hearing, sight and, more and more frequently, also speech. Now, in spring of 2002, there were days when she couldn't put a sentence together and her mind felt like "a wet string mop." We assured Mary that this project wouldn't require a lot of strenuous work on her part at all. We simply wanted to get down what we knew she already had stored in her brain—we imagined a series of interviews. We wanted to see the unblinking honesty and realism that had always characterized Mary's writing trained on her own experience of living into old age (she was 84 at the time) in a body compromised by a stroke. "I think life beyond 70 ... is an adventure so far largely unrecorded, unanticipated, unacknowledged," writes Carolyn Heilbrun in a recent issue of *The Women's Review of Books* devoted to aging.[1] How much less recorded and acknowledged is life beyond 80, especially by women writing with the acute political consciousness and self-awareness Mary had.

The interviews Verena and I imagined never took place. Shortly after our conversation about the book, Mary handed me the journal she'd just completed, suggesting I take a look and see if it contained anything worth excerpting. I began by marking what seemed pertinent passages, but realized about halfway through there was little in the book that wasn't pertinent. How to circumscribe the experience of aging, of living as an old person? Isn't attempting such circumscription—reducing old people to their limitations and complaints—the very essence of ageism?[2] Yes, the journal

1. Carolyn Heilbrun, "Taking a U-Turn: The aging woman as explorer of new territory," *The Women's Review of Books*, Special Issue: Women Aging, July 2003.
2. The most thoughtful and incisive writing on ageism I know is to be found in Barbara Macdonald and Cynthia Rich's pioneering collection of essays *Look Me in the Eye: Aging, Ageism*, first published in 1984 (Spinster's Ink Books). Mary was a great admirer of this book and reviewed it for *Trivia* when it was reissued in 1991.

was full of pungent observations about the humiliations and frustrations of living in an aging body. But Mary's attention was so inclusive, so global, that to extract from it that one thread would seem almost perverse.

In these notebooks—I soon asked to see all the ones she'd kept since her stroke—Mary wrote, was compelled to write, about all the lives being lived around her: friends, animals, caretakers, trees and plants. (Often she was compelled to draw them too; the pages were scored with fine line drawings, mostly of cats and flowers.) She wrote as much about the daily changes in the flame tree she saw from her window as she did about the changes taking place in her own body. Indeed often in her notebooks it seems the two threads are braided in her own mind: "The flame tree color can't be called faded. It's *sui generis* ... I have a fainting feeling in every cell. Falling scenarios. If I lean sideways I have to make a special effort not to keep going" (November 10, 2001). In these pages Mary also wrote about books, political events and the accelerating threat posed by human stupidity and greed, to the plants and animals she so loved. It did not take me long to realize that this was the book about old age we'd been envisioning—it was all right there.

My friendship with Mary began in 1988 at the International Feminist Book Fair in Montreal when I approached her wanting permission to publish the paper she'd just delivered, "Memories of Age." I was the editor of the feminist journal *Trivia,* at the time. Mary said yes and agreed to work with me on expanding the piece for publication. She was busy performing in *The Company of Strangers* that summer with the six other old women in the film, a thrilling experience for her, and the letters we exchanged in the following months often strayed far from editorial business. We continued to correspond once the piece was published—about feminist community, literature, our cats—and, after I moved to Montreal in 1990, the friendship deepened. At the same time, the editorial relationship continued, at least on an informal basis—we regularly shared our work with each other—and Mary almost always asked me to mark hers up. Now, having been handed the treasure of these notebooks, it seemed only natural for me to take on the task of editing them for publication.

What I did not foresee was that most of this editorial work would have to be done without Mary's input. She died in November of 2002, about eight months after Verena and I first proposed the book to her. As her friend, I was bereft; as her editor, I was left in the uncomfortable position of having to decide on my own what to keep and what to leave out. There were many challenges, among them the question of where to begin. After the stroke, Mary spent two months in rehabilitation at Catherine Booth Hospital and would spend many more weeks there in the year to come recovering from falls. She was also in and out of the Jewish General, once to have a pacemaker inserted and once for hip replacement surgery. Mary wrote steadily throughout these hospital stays—noting every detail of her environment, including therapists, nurses and other patients, and documenting her physical struggles. It was tempting to include some of the writing she did during this period, which was so often hilarious:

> SEPTEMBER 25, 2000. A dialogue between mind and index finger. Mind: "Lie down flat." Finger: "I don't hear you, I'm tired." Mind: (angrily) "Lie down flat." Rt. hand intervenes. R.H. is power-hungry, feels vastly superior to L.H., kibbitzes whenever possible, will reach over and push hot water spigot which left hand is pushing as hard as possible—shut, not a drop. "It would have gone on dripping, idiot," R.H. says. L.H.: "I'll show you, you tyrant." She has taken to pushing the left wheel of the wheelchair down the corridor to 202, this time with R.H.'s cooperation, not showing off but pushing slowly so wheelchair will go in a straight line. This is going better and better. The last turn in a circle near the red-striped fine rectangle is a tour de force, left hand holding wheel motionless, R.H. pushing hard. Wheelchair ends parallel to the wall and very close ... [3]

In the end I decided to resist this temptation and to focus solely on Mary's last years in her own surroundings. Between the end of 2000 and her death in late 2002, Mary was confined almost entirely to her home on Grosvenor Avenue, where, apart from a steady stream of caretakers and friends, her cats and the life in her garden were her constant companions. It seemed to me these last two housebound years formed a kind of container for Mary in which, consciously or not, she could begin the dying process. Many thoughts and dreams arose during this time about her twin sister Sarah and her brothers Arthur and Wister—all three of whom had died before her—and about the approaching end of her own life. She dreamt extraordinary dreams about wild animals, about her past and her diminishing physical powers.

Verena Stefan's reminiscence included in this volume provides many of the particulars of Mary's routine during this period. While she was in the hospital recovering from the stroke, a bathroom was installed on the ground floor of the house and a hospital bed set up in her living room. Later a big blue velour lift-assist chair replaced a living room wing chair. As she grew weaker, Mary's daily round consisted mostly of moving from that chair to the kitchen or to the dining room where she used the dinner table as her writing desk. It was, as Verena points out, a time of renunciation. Mary's journals testify to the struggle she had to wage to be present to her own life in all its limitation. "I have to make the most of a shrunken landscape," she

---

3. Excerpts from Mary's hospital notes, including this passage, were published in *The Capilano Review*, Series 2, No. 33, Winter 2001.

writes at one point. No doubt writing in the journals fortified her in this struggle, helping to anchor her here in her ailing body and in her house surrounded by objects of beauty and beings she loved.

Verena also writes of the challenge of providing home care for someone who jealously guarded her time alone. This challenge was complicated by the fact that Mary vehemently opposed the idea of hiring professional live-in help. In the first two years after her stroke, women from the Florida community of Sugarloaf Key, where Barbara Deming had lived the latter part of her life and where Mary had been spending part of every winter, came up to Montreal to care for her. They came from Florida, New Jersey, Alabama and Vermont, usually in shifts of one or two months at a time. When this arrangement became unmanageable, her closest friends urged her to consider hiring a nurse. Mary was adamant. She was willing to put up with a night nurse, but if she had to share her home with helpers during the day, she wanted them to be friends. At the time, some of us thought she was being unrealistic.

Mary had thought a lot about environments for aging and death. In a speech she was to give at an OLOC (Old Lesbians Organizing for Change) conference just around the time of her stroke, she touched on this subject, invoking as a model the community of Sugarloaf Key:

> The dying process today has become the subject of a vast field of study, in order to meet the needs, which have become big business, of the population of longer-living people. The ideal is to provide a setting of care and friendliness, with interests and activities that will prevent people in retirement homes from ever feeling bored or abandoned. To me the most successful of these environments falls short of the caring for dying friends in a lesbian community by a support group that views death as a final kind of sharing. Barbara Deming took us into her fear and pain toward the acceptance of her own death; so did Ruth Dreamdigger. Each of them took charge of her death surrounded by loving friends with such grace, such generosity of spirit that those friends and family who were present felt honored and included.
>
> The lesbian community at Sugarloaf Key, the one I know and admire for their sensitive attention to each other, has learned from experience that a dying friend's deepest need, even when she cannot speak, is to be listened to. In a retirement home family and friends cannot be present twenty-four hours a day, the staff may not have the time to calm the anxiety of dying, nor to recognize the lingering place between life and death when an apparent farewell to life can really be an awareness still of links to the living. Each of us hopes that we will be able to traverse this with the final tranquillity that the dying seem to experience in an atmosphere of love.[4]

4. *The OLOC Reporter*, Fall 1999.

At the time she wrote this piece I don't think it occurred to Mary that she would be calling on this same community of women in the very near future—or that she was surrounded by a similar community herself. Mary's longtime friends carefully considered her wish to be cared for by women she knew instead of professionals. Between them they managed to create a network of caretakers, most of them drawn from Montreal's community of lesbian writers and artists, and together, friends and caretakers worked out a system of alternating day shifts. The system worked. But it did more than work. As her journals attest, Mary's days from now on were filled with women who were not only exquisite caretakers but friends with whom she could carry on conversations about art, writing and political events, as well as about the garden, the cats and her physical condition. These women would continue to care for Mary until her death.

Mary's last years, from this point of view, were a time of abundance. If she could not always hear what was being said around her, she was "listened to" with the closest attention. Her senses of taste and smell, which seemed to have survived intact, were indulged at mealtimes when her caretakers took pleasure in serving up gourmet vegetarian creations. Though she could not leave her house, when she looked out her window she saw a garden that had been tended and coaxed into luxuriance. The presence of this community of women and the atmosphere of love and friendship they created in her home was another compelling reason to focus this book on the very last part of her life.

Mary's own creativity also flowered in these last two years, sometimes in new and surprising forms. In 2001 she began a regular correspondence with her lifelong companion Marie-Claire Blais in the form of faxes between Marie-Claire's cat Mouser and Mary's cat Miky. The faxes started up in late fall when Marie-Claire left Montreal for Key West and stopped when she returned to the city in spring, resuming in the summer months when she left for their country house in Kingsbury, Quebec. Mary's faxes were often richly illustrated and marked by a kind of loose humor and whimsy she rarely permitted herself in her other writing. Beginning in December 2001, the reader will find a selection of these faxes alongside her journals, appearing according to the date of transmission.

About a year after the stroke, I talked Mary into freewriting with me for the first time. The cardinal rule of freewriting is that you keep your pen moving, you don't stop to edit or correct. Mary had never tried writing this way before—which considering she'd written five books and tried her hand at every other kind of writing was mind-boggling to me—but once she got started she was hooked. We freewrote regularly together after that. We'd start with a line from a book of poetry and then just go ... for five or ten minutes. Then we'd start over again.

No matter how tired she was, or how foggy her brain, once Mary got going a spark would alight in her and something astonishing would almost always emerge from her pen. "Frustrated dormant worker bees in my head waiting for some reason to unlock the signal for life" is how she describes the process in one of her freewrites. In her journal she muses, "Strange how my turgid brain always seems to produce something that is faintly witty." After we'd finished a series of freewrites we would read them aloud to each other. There was always at least one line in each of Mary's pieces that made me laugh out loud (e.g.: "Warm encouragement strikes like a dead pancake"). But they were never only funny. Freewriting was an outlet for the poet and the sage in Mary. It was also yet one more way in which she registered the experience of living in an aging body. This volume includes a collection of Mary's freewriting—the record of her creative life in these last two years would not be complete without it.

—LISE WEIL

Beyond Recall

In a dream I asked, "Did you call?" I waited, I said your name over and over, you didn't answer or open the door. Are they refusals for all time? Though when you were alive there was that sudden bright look of recognition once, a gathering of your living being in greeting. That much my subconscious is willing to grant. If only we could force the deadlock, a tiny motion and the sound of something falling into place. Like winning the lottery. But we have to die first.

—Freewrite, May 29, 2001

Preface

My greatest difficulty at 85 is to think coherent thoughts. I want to think about old age and instead my blurry eyes are drawn away from this paper by the movement of spring leaves, yellow-green, outside the window. They have been tossed by the wind for days and have grown into darker green summer leaves that fill the red spaces of the brick wall behind. Today a flock of little white birds has settled near the top of the Dolgo apple tree in a horizontal ripple; they will be the blossoms that Sylvie predicted. The scrutiny of them deflects my thoughts from old age.

Is old age the ideal way to finish living? Monique Bosco in *l'Attrape-Rêves* speaks of "the only winter that counts, the long and rigorous winter of old age." I am pampered by sensitive women with generous hearts, who are artists, gardeners, inspired cooks, can listen without sighs of impatience to my croaky hesitant voice as I try to recall something or describe someone. To me my speech sounds as if I were a little drunk. I have trouble hearing properly both with and without my hearing-aid.

We should all have been seriously preparing for old age. Our bodies are in the process of choosing our death without telling us how it will happen. But like my mother and older brother I had a stroke and learned a new vocabulary of therapy and hospital life and medication. We learned in therapy classes how not to fall down and how to make it harder to forget. But falling down ambushes us, finds a new method for tipping us over that we haven't prepared for. As for forgetfulness, like an invisible, colorless, weightless gas, it may steal on us without warning, but the memory can't be bullied or coaxed back. What gladness I feel when a memory returns, unforgettably clear. It may bring back something trivial or the reality of a dear friend and the life of our friendship. Sometimes it stays for weeks, or sometimes, capriciously, it vanishes in the next minute.

I don't want to live to a great old age, losing my faculties according to the unknown time-table that controls our aging. Friends enthusiastically give me examples to follow of energetic women, who have lived to be 100. But that makes one think of the injustice of deaths died too soon. I still mourn for my father's death at 61 of tuberculosis just before penicillin became a cure. We were beginning to discover our closeness to each other, to realize how long it takes for children to catch up to their parents, to be accepted as friends.

We are encouraged now to prolong life as long as possible with hip and knee replacements, pacemakers, an array of medications. Some of us get a kind of negative pleasure from the number and severity of our ordeals. In the animal world death is sometimes programmed so that the new generation can take over. Salmon turn a glorious red and become part of the great food chain; cicadas which have just emerged from seventeen years underground, transformed now into nymphs, swarm on tree trunks and set up a deafening mating-song. In the din the females somehow choose the best singers; they mate, and lay their eggs in the bark of trees. How tragic human death seems compared to the cicadas' ode to joy and celebration of a new life, to the salmon's radiant color and leaping dance up rapids before they die. Sometimes human beings, too, celebrate the passage from life to death. My brother Wister's four children, when he was dying, gathered around him and sang the songs that they had always sung together.

Before my twin died I went to visit her in the retirement home where she and her husband were living out their lives. She did not talk much and sat in her wheelchair with her head bent low. I was almost unable to talk myself, guilty of being still well with nothing comforting to say, guilty of never having talked from the depths of my heart. Suddenly she looked up, straight at me. Her eyes were a clear green. "My Mary," she said. It still makes me want to sob—her face was so kind. So we forgave each other once and for all for the times when we followed the old pattern of mistrust, and failed to reach toward each other. Now I conjure up that old joy instead of futile regrets, the bane of old age.

My three siblings died in the order of their birth: 1996, 1997, 1998. I was ready to complete that sibling sequence, but the years have gone by and I'm still here, hugging my pessimism—mourning the deaths of my dearest contemporaries, mourning the disappearance of forests, birds, animals and fish.

Recently I watched a video my brother Arthur had made over a period of years. I saw myself and my siblings young, my nieces and nephews as infants struggling to walk, our futures still locked inside us. In my lifetime it has become possible to make the passage of time visible, to see ourselves growing up, growing old, moving toward death. My lifetime has spanned convulsions of violence, hate, genocide, a vision of Armageddon, against the quiet working of miraculous discoveries that bind the living world together at the very moment that it is being smashed to pieces. But no act of violence can change the fact that as human beings we share percentages of identical DNA with flowers, animals, worms, that the intuitions of poets and philosophers like Blake and Spinoza have been correct.

In the beautiful little world around me, this house and its garden moving in the wind, with my pleasant schedule and lovable friends, a heavy curtain sometimes seems to fall in me. The invisible particles that make decisions have been consulting again. "Let's try blocking dreams. Let's prevent an idea from becoming intelligible." My dreams continue but by the next day only fragments remain. They are images of a diminished creative state where even ten years ago I often heard real birdsong, the thrilling song of a scarlet tanager, for instance, and saw him on a tree top. Bluebirds, eagles, exotic birds I had never seen in life, acted as symbols of joy and I woke from these dreams feeling happy. Now only fragments remain from dreams full of strangers, unfamiliar cities and landscapes. Now and then there are points of light. The other night I saw my twin seated tranquilly in sunshine in a lawn chair. She didn't see me and when I woke up I thought I must stop begging silently for more than that. It is a new place beyond recall, where reproaches die and her silent tranquillity takes their place.

But I'm still going over evidence of my creative past: drawings, poems, projects for a book about old age or a book about being a fraternal twin.[5] With all this evidence to fill the blanks, memories swarm and flower in a kind of springtime. I want to stretch out my hand and capture a few recent memories like fireflies with their cool incandescence and let them go.

5. Shortly before her stroke in 1999, Mary and her editor and publisher at Talonbooks, Karl Siegler, had agreed her next book would be about her relationship with her fraternal twin, Sarah. That book exists in only a few scattered drafts and fragments—the scope and vision of it now "beyond recall." (See also page 24, journal entry of January 13, 2001.)

TO MY DEATH

I can measure you more or less
In years, you in the shadows
Of myself, and don't
I sometimes feel your
Fingers round my throat?
What is your intention?
Will you paralyse, or suffocate
Me or make me incontinent,
More and more absent-
Minded, will the unspent
Resentments of a life spill
Out, will you steal my will?
Make powerless my heart?
Torture me, give one
Of your long lessons in pain?
I have got off too easily,
You have hidden from me,
My death, bigger than my size
Like a mantis that eats its mate,
Age draws me to you in spite
Of myself. If only I knew
If some good part will outwit you.
Or, in pain
Will I complain and complain?
Will there be memory enough
In me to remember to love?

The Journals
&
Faxes

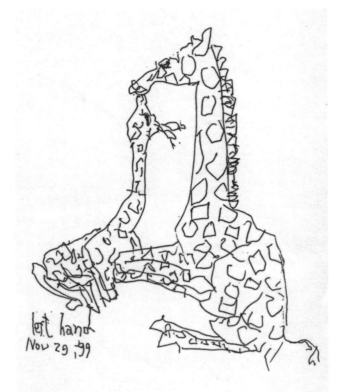

left hand
Nov 29, '99

JANUARY 2, 2001, TUESDAY. Yesterday sick paroxysm of guilt—about rudeness to J. or a kind of stunning negativity—no, I won't come to Key West this year; no, I don't think I'm getting better and better. Enraged by the sentimental optimism of the Québécois. But everybody is soothed by their own optimism. And this is the whole point of "How are you today?" "Good, thanks," the correct answer until the day she dies in *Wit*[6] ...

JANUARY 6. Verena[7] coming at 11. Am in a state of collapse, stupidity, words that come out haltingly ...

The strange metamorphoses of faces ... Have they changed or do my eyes turn them into different people? ... Looking at myself I see irreversible distortions, queer uncontrollable grimaces, the difficulty of moving my tongue to make words, of controlling my tongue, jaw, mouth when I'm eating. Have to dab at my mouth constantly. This gets worse with lots of talking. Slurred consonants. But still a certain clarity of thought.

JANUARY 8. Snowing in a determined way, fine. Stuck in its almost everyday habit. It starts—suddenly a lace curtain in front of my eyes. The hat on Gloria's statue is as high as ever but the snow has shrunk from around the base. Dr. A.'s office called & changed the appt. to next Tuesday. A lurching of the stomach. Without telling me why, of course. There is *no* consultation. Virginia Woolf & details—don't let them get away from you, she said to Nigel & Ben. What color were his socks? etc. ... Now—snow back—lit by sunshine lighting a white sky ... Used wrong number yesterday for my fax to M.C.[8]—Ann[9] too. Today right number ... but paper got scrumpled up and a piece of it is still in machine. A tantalizing tiny corner of it sticking out.

6. Margaret Edson, *Wit*, NY: Farrar, Straus and Giroux, 1993.
7. Verena Stefan. (See page 158 for a list of caretakers.)
8. Marie-Claire Blais, writer, lifelong companion.
9. Ann Pearson, photographer, college professor, longtime neighbor and friend. She volunteered to help Mary with bookkeeping in the last years of her life.

JANUARY 13. Terrible dreams ... 1) *Huge milling crowd of women, as close together as a school of fish. Weaving like a school of fish. They are trying to isolate Sarah and push her against a wall?* Horrible and scary. 2) 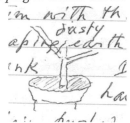 *Mother is standing in front of a table with different-sized terracotta flowerpots on it full of dry earth. There is a dead branched plant in one of them with thin pruned branches. She is heaping dusty earth around the central small trunk.* Depressing! Both ... seem to have awful significance— ... Sarah is being pushed out of memory inexorably. I have felt this lately, said to M.C. in fax that I don't have enough memories, can't retrieve them, to write a book. That her life story belongs to her children. Dixie, in fact, now has claim to it. Is it I being pushed against a wall? As for Mother and the dry earth—a dream about trying to bring the dead to life. Both suffocating. Maybe I'm really having difficulty breathing. Slight dizziness today and wobbly gait.

JANUARY 14, SUNDAY. Sleepy, rag doll feeling as though there were no muscles around my waist ... Colorless day. A clump of snow turtle-shaped on branch of Gloria's maple. Lily guided by me away from desk space has managed to disarrange all piled-up letters, top one slowly slithering toward me, propelled by her left paw.

JANUARY 20. Inauguration Day. Bush strutting confidently around, Clinton disappeared—and he seems loveable and totally alive compared to the poker-faced, carefully smiling Bush. (Bouchard, too, very likable now that he has resigned.) Dream. *I'm looking at a glassy blue-grey sea and know that it's wintry cold. But pairs of little boys are swimming calmly around in it. Then I'm in it with another woman, not swimming but walking slowly over the bottom. I want to swim but she is holding me down.* Meaning: she is the self who forces me to go so cautiously, who seems to hold me back ... When I wake up from these dreams I just barely make it to the bathroom. Some connection certainly—the nervousness about hospitalization, possible cystoscopy that keeps me awake, sometimes with a fine trembling. Yesterday Dr. G. stretched my mouth so wide that there is a red spot at each corner. And exhausted today—have started taking beautifully red iron tablets that have a nauseating effect.

JANUARY 22. Total collapse. Loose bowels, blurry eyesight. Compulsive tidying & retidying ... Verena —so soothing, unflappable, competent ... When she came I said, "I feel woozy today, V." So do I! She thought it was something in the atmosphere. Leonie had left the inner door locked and poor V. had rung, knocked and called while I struggled to get up, the chair slid back several times and I hobbled to the door.

JANUARY 26. Dream images of animals last two weeks. *1) I'm being pulled into a room by a big goat with curved horns and a coat like a pointer's, smooth grey and white, silvery 2) an image of two small snow-white hens about as big as pigeons. Beautiful! 3) Last night—I look down on the ground in the woods— somewhat spongy ground with bits of woods, etc. I see a golden beetle, about 3/4 inch, and pick it up between thumb & forefinger—smooth surfaced & almost round. It swells up and grasps me with hundreds of prickly legs. I wake up with my right hand asleep* ... Another dream that confirms my theory of the connection between dreams and waking states of the body. ... #3 A direct result of seeing an eighteen-foot female anaconda on TV swimming & then lying on the ground. Eight smaller males have coiled around her, attempting to mate. "To spread their genes," the narrator invariably says. She is wrapped almost her entire length with snakes. This was a beautiful documentary. Flat worms (rudibrachs?) face each other aggressively. Each has a protruding spike & attempts to get it into the other. Both are both male and female. The Apollo butterfly, white with black spots. The white like satin. The male mates & then plugs up the orifice with a wicked-looking hook, so that his genes will prevail (of course) and no other male can mate ...

Birds: peacocks, mandarin ducks, painted pheasants, their colors are incredibly beautiful. Brilliant red and black, green, ethereal blue. The brownish, unbeautiful female does the choosing, always the male with the most striking or perfect colors, who must do non-stop mating with all the eager females. Both sexes seem to be preoccupied with spreading their super-genes and perpetuating the race. In the Kiwi race the male is bigger but the female can contain an immense egg that almost fills her body ... The sad tale of the lion who kills every cub not his—why? A threat to his perfect genes. Human beings can be just as selective but fortunately don't kill the children of the new wife by her first husband. Blue-footed boobies are happily unfaithful to their mates when the mates go off fishing. Why are booby genes spread around? I forget.

January 31. I don't feel quite as awful today but still feeling wobbly, even shuffling my left foot (no brace) plus the sensation of not having any muscles, perhaps being the strawman in *The Wizard of Oz*. And making any effort—to open the tiny box of Neocolors that Joanna gave me, to dip one into water—seems beyond doing, and interruptions to my writing the kind of bullet that explodes & shatters. Lily, after knocking the calendar onto the floor, is arranged with her head on a pile of envelopes and her chubby paw hooked under it—wing of ear whisker & lovely nose-whiskers while high-lighted right paw propped back on left one.

FEBRUARY 3. 3/4 of Lily spread 6 inches away from me her whiskers delicately curved over my pewter sea urchin, knife on top of scratch pads. When she moves a great clatter to the floor will take place.

Feb. 3, 81

FEBRUARY 4. A few seconds ago Lily almost succeeded in getting from the typing table to my most vulnerable pile of mail after grand tidying. The hot feeling & the heavy resistant pressure of atmosphere. As if deep underwater ... The time with Lise was inebriating ... —I was hot and excited after doing 3 or 4 freewritings in a kind of trance—paradoxical and funny things that magically flowed out. Slightly shattered when Ann came at her usual time to do useful financial things ...

FEBRUARY 5. Slippage of time ... Today, first a comfortable relaxed feeling in bed, L. had put the pillow close to my back so that it held me on my side and for once I didn't want desperately to pee. Got up at 6:45, surprised to find my back aching, my knees wobbling, & taking the same faltering steps. And with the familiar overcooked spaghetti feeling. A kind of vagueness behind my eyes. How much is the effect of Didrocal? ... I have the instant blowing-up feeling, small sharp pains in various parts of my body, *heat* (the usual) but appetite quite voracious.

FEBRUARY 7. On blue pill now & don't see much difference. Still blowing up in puffs—mistaken idea that there will be instant change & energy. Yesterday usual tizzy over snow. Cabdriver parked with slushy place near curb to walk through & a stretch of sidewalk to navigate ... In the middle of the night I woke up & couldn't think how to say I needed the bedpan. Today the total Collapse ... A sort of headache, prickly eyes & runny nose ... Started

Eva Hoffman[10] at breakfast ... The instant lifting of spirit, Hoffman's first sentence. What is it about living words, where is this life, or where isn't it? What is left out? Too secret, too carefully discreet? Is that something I can say or does M. imagine a life in her writing that isn't in herself? She is full of knowledge, huge amounts of research, accurate perceptions of human beings. Very strange ... I remember a time when words didn't fit exactly— too big or too small or too dark or heavy or light. In last part of *The Time Being*[11] sluggish words full of audible effort, not intentional. For there is always a way of making a heavy state buoyant.

FEBRUARY 8. Dentist day, CLSC[12] day. Waiting for CLSC Coumadin blood sample. Already in a nervous state. Raindrops on screen ... Eva H. has the power to be present and detached at the same time. The violence is always simply stated, matter-of-factly. Men beat their wives. Exists as a brutal *present* fact. Her language is unadorned, but it carries its own weight of joy or tragedy or humour ... Her parents' lifestyle flowering from the facts of politics and life in Poland after the war. They live risky and happy lives.

FEBRUARY 10, SATURDAY. Dream. *I'm running to catch a train, holding the hand of a young slim happy-looking young woman. A big station like the one in Washington long ago. Suddenly I realize that I've forgotten my shoes, turn back and start running back, get lost, meet another young woman wearing glasses, not beautiful. I come to the station; there are two tracks going in opposite directions running under a metal corrugated roof, with a busy road running between, trucks, vans, etc. passing on it. On the other side I see a bus or a train with a sign in front saying MONTREAL. I want to cross the road to get to it and look up and down to see if there's an opening. There's nothing big enough. I wake up wanting acutely to pee.* This seems to have been dreamed because I want to pee and is also about youth, age, infirmity. My swift smooth running is impeded by the indifferent brutality of traffic. (The second young woman is wearing glasses & is unbeautiful.) Do I find my shoes? I can't remember ... Deathless sentences in my head last night when I was waiting for Eliz. have faded away.

FEBRUARY 11. -20° today, cloudless sky—to be even colder tonight. Lily in exactly the same position as yesterday with lovely fat paw extended & white whiskers delicately lying across it. Schumann playing CBC and I'll never

10. Eva Hoffman, *Lost in Translation*, NY: Penguin Books, 1989.
11. *The Time Being* was Mary's most recent book, published by Talonbooks in 1997.
12. *Centre local des services communautaires*, a community health clinic.

learn really to love him—repetitions? I hardly dare mention such a word even to myself. Must ask someone who won't scoff. But Beethoven is complex all the time except when exquisite melody sings as in 110. And Shostakovich's chamber music is like this, too ...

FEBRUARY 15. A horrible feeling of limpness after the somewhat night-marish appointment with the urologist apparent monster who didn't look at me or acknowledge me in any way & talked only to the nurse who tried vainly to include me. "Miss Meigs is a very intelligent talented woman," she said. No answer. It was only when I said the cystoscopy I had 50 years ago hurt abominably that he looked at me. "It doesn't hurt. I've done about 1,000 cystoscopies and no one has complained of it hurting." Subject closed ... This morning at 4? insomnia, and I took the tiny piece of Serax I'd providentially put aside. Fell asleep & dreamt unrecoverable dreams. And I seem to be rowing against a swift tide & feel the anxiety of what seem like stroke symptoms: blurry eyesight, floating after-images.

FEBRUARY 16. Carole and her elegance in the great Kanuk coat. It gave me an idea of how I must have looked when I was thinking that I looked lumpish & unchic. This supposed mirror image has dogged me since childhood. Only rarely have I felt elegant (in my pink red Cardin cut velvet jacket & suedy silk pink shirt (*Company of S.*[13] festivities)—but always big sensible Mephisto shoes sticking out below narrow pants ...

FEBRUARY 17. M.C. thinks it may be the antibiotics that make me feel so awful. Have put on my brace again as a precaution and go at a slow crawl. Right hand trembles and handwriting is uncertain. Or is it Didocal? Every day after taking it I have the same symptoms of flatulence and the absolute malaise of my abdomen. Plus an urge to eat heartily together with stomach hard as a drum ...

FEBRUARY 19. When I woke up I thought this will be a good day. Then I took my pills and the antibiotic and the horrible feeling of overpowering slowness crept into me so that it now takes an effort to lift my pen and write correct words ... the way my mind works—the way one pushes a darning

---

13. *The Company of Strangers*, an award-winning National Film Board movie which Mary participated in. She recounted the experience in her book *In the Company of Strangers*, published by Talonbooks in 1991.

needle through a piece of thick material? I still think the oiled bird image is the most exact ... Note that I can write a sensible sentence but it creeps word by word instead of flowing.

FEBRUARY 22. Royal Vic Thursday.[14] ... The day nurse was tyrannical and nasty. I was sitting in a chair with plastic bags piled near me, ready to go, and said, "Do you want me to get out of the room?" "*Sit in that chair,*" with maximum meanness. I instantly hated her. She used this tone to all the patients. V., as always, with total efficiency managed our departure, wheelchair pushed by nice black man with POSSESSION T-shirt. COLD! ... Joy and the usual nagging sense of crankiness when I got home, telephone calls to be made, mail to be endlessly opened, total exhaustion from insomnia. More snow, piled up back and plastered over front, more snow coming tomorrow and Monday. Snow, the recurrent terror of my winter ... Yesterday a real tizzy brought on by the enormity of the Eldercare bill went on into the night and kept me awake from before dawn to 6:45 ... Glad not to have spasms. E. brought me 1/4 Serax.

FEBRUARY 24, SATURDAY. Started liquid iron which right through the closed top had a revolting smell. Laced with very sweet syrup and not bad at all, but glad to brush my teeth. Yesterday I hated myself, the picky querulous fear-ridden person, insensitive, ungrateful. Thought about people comparing themselves to beasts: pigs, dogs, etc., unloading their own worst selves on animals, their *most human* selves. "I behaved like a beast." Last night Lily was sleeping in the tall armchair, had quietly claimed it. Miky eyed her balefully ... then jumped up, pounced on her and started roughing her up. A hue and cry, Lily on her back, Miky seriously tearing at her pale belly fur. Lily freed herself with a loud squall and leapt away. Gratuitous human-type jealousy and pure meanness. Miky's eyes turn yellow with cold rage.

FEBRUARY 25. Dream. *I'm in an open old-fashioned? train station, a platform without any roof over it and a long bench with people seated the whole length and black leather satchel-duffel type bags piled up at the end. Aunt Sarah is seated at the other end* ... This morning at breakfast I read Eva H.'s wonderful pages about coming to Vancouver from Cracow. Her nostalgia. The kind of piercing and vivid nostalgia that is transformed into a special sensuous memory that gives life to everything one lives afterwards and becomes the

---

14. Throughout most of the winter of 2001 Mary travelled twice weekly to the Ross Pavilion of Royal Victoria Hospital for physiotherapy.

ideal ... Now I think Sarah and I were like foreign children except for our common language. We were completely ignorant of popular music and the rest of popular culture, we dressed weirdly, i.e. plain serge dresses with changeable white collars, plain shoes or boots ... There was no question of having boyfriends though I remember that a couple of the plainer & more friendly ones climbed over the fence & pranced around in the back yard. They were never invited into the house. Memories of all this don't create joy. The Peak, Woods Hole and Naushon create the whole spectrum of bliss and smell comes back as sharply & with painful nostalgia as sight & taste & touch. Just came. Comtuit in a tremendous NE storm, the waves roaring up the beach, the spray dashing against the windows, the violent noisy shudder of the house, the smell of the sea. Sarah and I are put to bed. And glee when the sun breaks through the clouds and radiant patches of bluest sky. Addie has been mopping.

FEBRUARY 26. Temp. 2° C. but going down again. Pale sun filtered through pale clouds. No snow on G.'s sundial, a lop-sided phallic symbol about to fall over? ... At 6:30 decided to get up. I thought it would be nice to have lots of time for deskwork. Everything went wrong: first, a surprise BM threatened to mess everything up, then, hot cereal thickening in no time, sticking, extra steps, still can't find jam, probably right in front of my nose, honey all over everything, wobbly walk, reluctant stodgy brain, iron solution spills from spoon, prolonged BM. I finally get to work-table at 9:55. Eva H. wonderful, though, about life in Vancouver when she was 14 & her father tried to start a junk business. The difference between teenagers in Cracow & Vancouver. The shallowness of Canadian teenagers, their deliberate artifice, her radio talk about the boringness of Vancouverites and life there. Her incompatibility with grand scenery, the meeting of the Rockies & the ocean. My memories of identical feelings Sarah and I used to have about our peers—superiority, total difference. And the severity of immense mountains, how much more friendly fields, pasture & wildflowers & cows are ...

Man from "Wheelchair Sports Association" called. Me: I don't want to be telephoned. W.S.: "We're not telephoning, we're verifying your address." Wanted me to pledge $50 immediately. I said very loudly that I didn't want to be telephoned. My impression of a pit bull with his teeth fastened in my ankle. I shout "I'm hanging up," and do ...

FEBRUARY 28. Yesterday—sheer ice, helped across by Eliz. ... Verena sprinkled a lot of cat litter before I got home from therapy and Michel held on to me ... Total instability of mind and body today. Cynthia[15] dropped in and polished off the Balvenie; we talked about my possessions, what she'd like; I promised her little bone & wood spinning goddess (bathroom), blue cashmere Indian scarf, she spoke of love for white wings ... The business of possessions, deciding before I die, puts everybody in an uncomfortable position, including me—my friends feel grasping & I feel instantly possessive ... After she left I hurried fatally to be ready for Eliz., did everything wrong, buttoned pajamas wrong, couldn't get new Polartec jacket and denim shirt off, trouble with getting left leg into left pajama leg. Now—hot head, slight headache ...

MARCH 3. This morning -20° C. A big jump from last time. Exhaustion after Thursday therapy. My usual nervousness about ice in front, surly cab driver, warmed up in course of trip to Ross, made conversation even before tip (I'd said, "It's scary for old people to walk on ice." Made him think? Horrible winter for cab drivers?) Cold goes on. Bright sun. G.'s statue still has snow on it. Undulating snow on porch stairs over a foot deep. Alberta spruce greenish.

MARCH 4. Another COLD -15° C day. Yesterday morning an awful inadvertent BM and it took a whole hour to undress, wash, wash underpants, put on clean clothes, in course of which dabs of shit got on Polartec pants, underpants had to be rinsed in toilet and then thoroughly in sink, Polartec pants taken downstairs by V. and washed in set tub. Vigilance all day and this morning. Last night V.'s precautions against involuntary BMs only partially successful. Mashed potatoes, no beans, custard, V.'s invention, for dessert ... Big holes in memory now and inability to sustain ideas. Verena nudging me toward twin book, Lynda Hall nudging me toward more pages about the lesbian body, Beth Follett nudging me toward reading her mss. & writing a blurb & my reaction of no, no, no.

MARCH 5, MONDAY. A big blizzard has hit or is about to hit East U.S., Jovette[16] says Eastern Townships late morning and is coming early with *femme tellurique*. And I have an incomprehensible, perverse wish that the

15. Cynthia Scott, director of *The Company of Strangers*, friend and neighbor.
16. Jovette Marchessault, writer, sculptor, old friend. *La femme tellurique* is one of her sculptures.

blizzard will hit Montreal. Just to prolong our misery? Delay spring some more? Make it impossible to get to therapy? But that's almost never impossible ... At night, my mind teeming with ideas, in the morning they've disappeared & my brain is turgid. Only Eva H. fires it off, her wonderful pages about her Texan, the subtlety of her differences from him, how they can go on knowing each other better but will never know each other—the kind of intuitive knowing I have with many women but no men, with some nieces ... but no nephews, *never*—long ago—with the men who wanted to marry me ...

MARCH 11. Claudia arrived from NYC and England by plane & Greyhound bus ... cheerful, brimming with her usual imperturbable spirit, Miky looks up at her with round glowing eyes of love and hope. Here is a friend who can be counted on always to coo to him, never to be cool, unnoticing like me. Though yesterday he spent quite a long time in my lap in the blue chair with his front paws on my bosom not quite clasping my neck. Shoved him off the bed around 5 AM. My heart bleeds unyieldingly. Too bad he represents the male will and I represent the female refusal. Started Monique Wittig's piece on gender this morning. Dazzling clarity ... The phallic symbol has melted down to the grey statue, bird bath below still full of snow ...

MARCH 12. Bright sunshine and the same mini-mountains of snow on the back steps and pushing against the still blonde fence one foot below the top but G.'s sculpture only covered around bottom ...
Lily is lying head first in space between blue
bowl (exquisite sea grapeleaf mauve pink, signed by all Sugarloafers on top) and table edge, left paw stretched straight out, right paw in shadow of blue bowl ...

MARCH 18, SUNDAY. ... Ineptness with pen, with words, with lines and movements—this morning, too. Small muscles like flaccid or tightening elastic bands. Wrote Leonie's names wrong on check. Still wrong in my head. A muddle of pills, calcium pill mixed with iron syrup. Yesterday C. candled both ears—right in afternoon, left after supper, and cotton soaked with oil before candling. A hollow sound and crankiness. C. patient and calm ... My psychic level is horribly flat—worse when C. is depressed and without the buoyant cheer she has when she's happy. And it's self-centered and abject always to think it's my fault ...

MARCH 21. Cystoscopy. A longish wait—wheeled in, doctor and two nurses surveyed situation, then doctor, the one with stubbly beard and thick hairy arms, a piratical or biker-looking person, put his big arms under me and lifted me bodily onto table. General laughter. Stirrups. *Very cold* cream (to wash?) then even colder anaesthesia stuff applied, something put in, hurts but not unbearably. I say, "I have to pee." Dr.: "Wait a minute, I'll do it for you." He does something that makes the wish to pee disappear. Miraculous! He does some more foraging, painless, says, "O.K. it's all done. I can't see anything wrong so make an appointment in 6 months." ...

The swimming under water opaque feeling today. My drawings of Lily get worse and worse. Slowing-down mind. Determined snowflakes very small now, creeping up near top of fence, slowly covering Gloria's statue and sundial. I try not to think about birds. Usually the bluebirds and robins are here by March 22.

MARCH 24. A brilliant day and a snow-cover thrown over the fence. Two squirrels popping up and down in the depths—I thought were birds. Fence top hidden for a stretch of 20 feet. Uneven blobs falling off the trees. Maple buds fattening on tree. Little snow-pats clinging to the flame-bush ... Slow motion, shuffling gait specially right leg and knee, and slow moving mind. ... Need badly some freewriting with Lise. The horrible fear of having my mind snipped in two and my speech reduced to incomprehensible sounds ... The shadow of the apple branch released from a blob of snow (I just saw it fall) bounces up and down on the rosy, greyish brick wall. Writing saves me ... One peace lily out, immaculate, the chalice of the flower against the bright outdoor light. The flower is darker but holds light—its own kind.

MARCH 25. The same kind of brilliant day, minus something, house cold ... My mind moving at a snail's pace ... The Alberta spruce is a dull browny-green, and my spirits are the same color. I can't seem to feel light-hearted. Supposing the snow goes on all summer? Like the summer in 1828? I must change my rhythm, the days that repeat themselves, that don't know how to describe themselves, have a built-in forgetting and repetition. Only eating feels animated, and reading. I'm cold in my skin.

MARCH 30. The tips of the fence-posts are showing—about four inches out. Snow lower on steps. A still, colorless day ... How does Claudia do it—her spontaneous cheerful talk that can reach everybody including the cats. Miky gives an adorable little vocal response, opens his mouth a little and emits a soft miaow ... At therapy I want to throw my arms around the necks of all the staff but they look busy and seem to walk briskly by me. But Linda delighted me last week by embracing me & saying, "Take care of yourself, will you? Take care of yourself." Warm & loving. And Tamila was in one of her lightly flirtatious states, taking blood & a urine sample—has to crunch awkwardly behind me (on the commode) and wait until I pee, turns on the tap provocatively—it works—"I guess you'll be glad when you don't have to come here anymore." "Well it's a struggle to get here but it's nice when I'm here" ... Today I feel awful, achy.

April 6. ... A blunder yesterday talking to Zelda N. We were both protesting against Bush and his stupidity. Then we somehow got onto the subject of cultural atrocities. Every country has one she said. We talked about clitoridectomies. She said it would never change; I said it was changing. I said I'd seen a film about circumcision and the baby was screaming terribly. She said she had two sons and they'd been circumcised when they were 2 days old. As soon as they're back in their mothers' arms they stop crying. She was Jewish, she said. So I immediately feel officious, smart-aleck, etc. and still plan an apology.

April 7, Saturday. Lovely sunshine after light snow yesterday afternoon. Sandy & C. have gone up to Iranian store to get cheese for sandwiches. My eyes are very bad today, both of them. Reading glasses, eye migraine with. This morning 6:15 I practiced remembering words—the missing ones: circumcision—in my conversation with Zelda. Forgetting a form of punishing myself? Oppoponax. An exercise to combat short-term memory loss—without reason, can go on for a day or two, then come back. Tortures me with the possibility of having senility—gradually creeping up on me. Writing helps. Practicing words helps. Reading helps all this in the immediate—which vanishes. Can be reread, rehearsed.

April 13, Wednesday. ... The psychological drama of Theresa yesterday and my churning emotions, guilt feelings, feeling of being caught in an anticipated trap, of being on trial & not doing well, of behaving just as Mother and Sarah would have, though they might have behaved quite naturally (in a way that Theresa would accept). But for Mother the combination of lesbian & beard? My scenarios—being taken by T. to the dentist or doctor. "But Theresa is so calm, so used to these situations that they are calm, too," says Sandy, who has been silent most of the time ... She seems to be watching me sink into quicksand but she is really quietly letting me say what I think & how ashamed I am of how I feel. To say our familiar prejudices like a ventriloquist's puppet. To feel *compelled* to say things I hate hearing.

APRIL 16, MONDAY. Fax yesterday from Suniti[17] and I'd spent all morning writing one to her ... She had written a beautiful poem about a swan inspired by Mallarmé's *"le vièrge, le vivace et le bel aujourd'hui."* Suniti swims (or flies) so easily in the medium of poetry. I suddenly remember the very dark shadow of a pigeon close to the ground scooting rapidly over the snow yesterday ... The state of my pacemaker, grey and surroundingly swollen. Seems to explain my current woes—wobbly with intermittent foggy vision ... Cold in house and my noon cold state has come over me. A slight dread at the thought of the shampoo Sandy is about to give me ... She has pulled her beautiful hair back in a ponytail. The hope that she won't have it cut.

APRIL 23. Lily, nose pointing toward me, 1 inch from camelbone letter opener. My blurry state has begun, eyes & mind. Yesterday my hypochondria state about stroke symptoms & I gave S. names of friends to call if I have to be taken to Emergency & can't talk. I just noticed that I was in the same state on Feb. 15—after appt. with urology doctor ... who seemed so gruff and ageist and turned out to be very nice. This time a prolonged & extreme hot flash ... Also conviction of every conceivable symptom such as thudding heart or extreme heat or bad forgetful lapse. (Is Milly's name really Molly?) This forgetfulness comes with foggy eyesight—and may have nothing to do with eyes? ... Warm pink sunlight on every twig in garden facing me. Maple tree dark with bursting buds. Bright green patches of juniper, yew & spruces peeking through fence & step railings. Lily so quiet & well-behaved, hasn't pushed into work-space ... Winter, the winter state of siege, has slipped so quietly away, only a tiny patch of snow between steps & fence. Next day— gone.

APRIL 25. A quiet pale sunny day, cooler than yesterday. Gloria's tulips in orderly horizontal ranks at the end of her garden behind frog and sundial ...

Dream. *A lovely one-storey wooden house in a warm, dry semi-tropical forest with rather sparse trees. A couple lives here, the man is a famous writer, he has a tanned, rugged face and thin muscular body. He sits cross-legged (somewhat like Sandy) and utters wise statements now and then. I'm extremely anxious to be*

17. Suniti Namjoshi, poet, friend.

liked by him. I feel self-conscious, feel that everything I say is stupid. (Like my state with Eleanor[18] and Sherry[19]). Then we're leaving the house, walking barefoot on a road covered with thick, soft golden dust. At one point I realize that I've forgotten my pocketbook but that it's too late to go back for it (and I've forgotten the way?) We come up to an open truck stopped in the road, people in it. I realize that this part is being filmed. The scene is about how a message can be passed between people without speech or signals. The message is that they like us (or perhaps me?). I can see it passing between three people with only the gesture of one turning to the other ... I woke up and lay in the state of semi-sleep necessary for remembering dreams, rehearsing the dream over and over again until it does a kind of setting like gelatin. Even so I've lost a lot of it. Specially at the end.*

Sharon[20] (coming Friday) is depressed because her mother, 88, is having serious memory loss ... This ending of life by forgetfulness like a leisurely execution. Which of us has it spared at the Royal Vic? ... The 90-year-old woman who lives on Victoria Ave.? The woman who talks all the time in a deep voice and whose smile turns suddenly on and off like my flashlight. I'm just barely hanging on. This morning I realized I'd forgotten the existence of the beautiful little weed-pot (Sandy calls it) from the crafts fair (*de l'artisanat*), recognized it and its lovely grey-blue glaze and panel of crossed decoration. What sticks in the mind and why? And yet I remember *where* to find things and direct Sandy accurately right to the spot ...

APRIL 28. Post birthday full of flowers, telephone calls, a fax & trout & asparagus and crème brulée brought by Ann ... The friction between R. and me, what causes it? My face turns bright red with mysterious indignation ... R. to Sandy: "Does she need to go to the bathroom?" The fact that she addresses all her conversation to S. in a low (to me) voice so that I stop listening. Do I have the right to expect people to talk a little louder? This must be the plaint of all deaf people. And why don't I *try* to use my hearing-aid? The feeling of being aggrieved when I have *no right to be* ...

Bill (tall, graceful, close-cropped white beard) gave me a little box of Ricola pearls, soothing cough drops, small, hollow on one side, rounded on other. He exclaimed with joy when he saw my Macmillan's set of James and Chekhov. He said it was the first time he'd seen them in someone's library. He noticed *Lucy Gayheart* and wants to give me *The Professor's Daughter*. I

18. Eleanor Wachtel, radio interviewer and friend.
19. Sherry Simon, professor of French Studies.
20. Sharon Batt, writer, breast cancer activist, friend.

said O.K. if you'll let me give you *Lucy Gayheart*. He talked very lucidly about the virtues of Cather's writing ... He talked about Turgenev—strange because my set was all down in the cellar—and I said, in a state of bad self-consciousness, "Do you know that Edmund Wilson compared Morley Callaghan to Turgenev? What do you think?" I turned red, shook with nervousness. Morley Callaghan seemed much dryer than T., he said, not so satisfying, left him wanting something ... I agreed but didn't know why. Can't remember any of either. Is remembering significant, does it mean something about a writer's power (I can remember James' novels, even a lot of the names).

APRIL 30. Dream. *Sarah, Mother and I are seated at a table. Mother has been scolding us for something but I don't remember for what. Sarah looks across at me and says calmly, "You've been nagging, Mama. You've been nagging." I admire the absence of any irritation or emotion in her voice. Mother begins to cry, a tear rolls out of the left corner of her left eye. I ache with sorrow for her and lean toward her to touch her face, embrace her tenderly ... Obvious that I can be all three of us.*

MAY 1. Glorious day warming up. Just went out, heaving walker over doorsill, catching wheels in cracks between boards, to look at rhododendron. Is it turning green? I send it strong greening wishes. Something like the fading grey over my pacemaker—the life inside working slowly, making things right ...

MAY 4. Nose running, bad cough, temp. 100° ... Last night horrible. Heavily awake for hours, nausea-feeling. Got up to go to bathroom and left knee buckled repeatedly, inched my way along ... Eyes bad, left one small & itchy. Vision not good. Depressed ...

MAY 9. ... Still feel vaguely sick and unsteady as if a weight inside my head were off center and pulling it down. Like a huge ball-bearing loose & rolling around. A loose cannon—huge metaphor for something that creates its own crazy momentum. I blame the antibiotics ... Meantime the garden in the shadowless light is splendid, the Dolgo snow-white, every tone of green, the roses (2) sprouting at last & the rhododendron with its slow spring life regulating its pace. Will it flower this year?

Yesterday late afternoon I wrote: essentially Ross Pavilion notes ... Such compassion I felt for *us*, the old ones on the bus, all of us who are no longer all there, who stagger along on walkers or canes (only Mme. X walks quite briskly and the one with the beautiful blue raincoat who smiles at me— firmly she walks—with determination) ... The school supervisor whispered "90" when I asked him his age: rugged scratchy face like a walrus' skin, wisps of hair, talks softly about what's going on in the world, the terrors, the horrors ... He forgot things he said. No longer with it. His voice kept dropping to a whisper, I couldn't hear ... The woman next to me had dentures, seemed blue all over, the beautiful blue raincoat, blue eyes, a big friendly smile, didn't talk. She was deaf in her left ear. Then suddenly she would answer some question of mine. "De Maisonneuve," she said. That was where she lived. This time I had to grope my way past her (Grosvenor came first). Almost fell down ... Now, later, cool in the house and Lise's heart-warming message echoing in my mind. She praised my hospital notes which I said were like "skimmed milk." A surge of faith, hope, the power of self, this transformation which has happened all my life long. It seems like my real self but in fact, is the person at the other end of the see-saw. Yesterday saw a very glossy spotted starling foraging in the grass.

MAY 12. Cool, lightly rainy, everything in garden more cheerful, Dolgo blossoms almost fallen, rhododendron *blooming*, still a rather dark green, Gloria's maple has recovered, leaves no longer limp. Can't see weeping juniper. Strange that the brown blight always strikes after its wonderful coming to life ... The miracle of rain.

MAY 14 Cool and sunny, still, leaves gleaming in sunshine. A wish to correspond to this brightness, to feel the lightness of being, a little song in every word. Instead I'm conscious of my body & its sluggish weight, its reluctance to move with that unselfconscience it used to have. But did it ever have it? Now some heavy element like mercury seems to run in my veins and affect my balance. Depression. But there's nothing specific to be depressed about—except my constantly runny nose. An embedded allergy, residue of shingles. I have to make the most of a shrunken landscape ...

Last night I woke up around 4 AM, used bedpan, couldn't get back to sleep, twisted in bed, heaved pillow to other side. L. watching (she sees me looking at my watch around 6, no matter how covert I am). I think about pocket pets, the irresistible bushbabies, hundreds die as pets without a proper habitat. The crime of this egotistic human arrogance makes me ache. I think of Odette and her bushbaby in Africa, can't remember how long it lived ... Her calm certainty that she knew what was best for it ... Dolgo apple tree has lost all its blossoms. Peonies? Hidden behind French lilac ... One peace lily stiff as a poker, two gently bent near top of stem, leaves joyfully green. Heavenly greens outside; I wish Verena would come. Just read all my freewriting and really liked.

MAY 14, AFTERNOON. 4 PM. Storm clouds and cumulus clouds replace each other. Bright sunshine with storm clouds and shadow with blue sky. My nose feels stuffed up, coldy but have done stairs and getting up and sitting down ... Blowing leaves reflected obliquely in kitchen window. Conjunction of sun, cloud, wind, stillness, blue pushing at white cloud at stormy clouds, like this week merging into next week. Energetic rustling of leaves.

MAY 15. Sunny windy quivering leaves beating up the sunlight ... Alma just found my BCI pen in the red wooden pen holder where Ann had put it. I was just accusing her of having put it *somewhere*—i.e. unfindable by me. And indeed *any* change means it's unfindable by me. The ability not to see something in front of your nose is something like memory loss—a total absence. On the phone with Lise I wanted to tell her about my solitary freewriting. A blank—running into a wall of fog? No suggestive word. As soon as I hung up everything came back in a seamless whole: *The Wreck of the Deutschland*, the 5 nuns, Hope's greying hair. A feeling of happy relief. Like a cat throwing up an intact mouse, still alive ...

Lily's head is between wide-spread paws—one of her beguiling positions ...

right index finger — The same temptation for stuffed-up nose) resist; eye hurts anyway. Lily's head is between wide-spread paws — one of her be-guiling positions. ... I realized that

MAY 19. Cool damp grey. I start thinking about one's insistence on remembering humiliations, refusals, puttings-down. Invertebrate like rudibrachs but armed with a deadly dart. The enemy is the self-reliant self who crumples up, who is ingested along with the dart. Voice: *you* think you're worthy to be in B.M.C.'s[21] archives but no one else thinks so. The desire to punish B.M.C., to withhold money. Voice: this would be cheap revenge. This dialogue can grind on for hours ... Oh, for someone to talk to. I forgot to bring it up with Verena. The virtues that I see in my work: drama, color, passion ... are old-fashioned virtues and don't count in contemporary art. Michel Brisebor is one of the few people left for whom they *do* count. And I'm lucky to live up here and to have the support of M.C. Indeed (the voice turns on) without it your illustrations would probably be worthless. (But, fortunately they are good, says the other voice, the one who believes in oneself.)

The lightly dancing leaves after the rain, sky brightening very slowly, rhododendron holding out a new arm with two mauve flowers at the end. Yesterday a wave of pain when I saw the shrunken yew. Draconian pruning, I said to Verena, but necessary ...

MAY 21. Victoria Day. A photo in *The Gazette* of Princess Louise's bronze statue of her mother the queen as a young woman. A wonderful fluidity of billowing skirts. Expressive face. Is she covered with pigeon droppings? My eyesight and hearing get worse and worse.

Dream. *I have to catch a train. The only way to get to the platform is to clamber up the side of a sort of chimney by iron handholds. The city is below. I get up one storey and am starting up the next when I wake up. Feeling of anxiety and fear.* This comes from climbing the stairs yesterday, the handholds, the feeling of effort and insecurity.

An ongoing argument about the garden ... Deadlock on the subject of impatiens. A hospital flower, I say, *des mauvais souvenirs*. I've turned sharply against all those massed colors, so happy in the heat and drought. They can stand anything and flourish. They don't change, they're like a stage set. Other flowers bud and bloom, have their season, even sweet alyssum and lobelia seem to move, lobelia specially, makes bright points of luminous blue. I feel homesick for the raised bed Jovette made for me next to my studio door at Sims.[22] The lobelia continued to flower all summer—deep

21. Bryn Mawr College. Mary was a '39 graduate. Shortly before her death, she donated her personal papers and three series of watercolor illustrations to the B.M.C. archives.
22. Mary and Marie-Claire's country home in Kingsbury, Quebec.

gentian blue, and a deep pink dianthus. Lots of white pebbles. And I can't rejoice in all the changes that are being made, M.C. happily telling me how M.M. has made my studio into a dwelling, hung pictures everywhere, etc. Spleen. Waves of spleen ... And ... D. wants my beautiful blue, red-lined cupboard that's on the wall. And a table. Grave robbery, extreme defensive reactions. Instead of calmness, generous sentiments, an attitude of so-be-it.

MAY 23. Light rain turning the porch steps dark. Lily wedged between chocolate box full of letters and stack of letters on Lori's bowl. M.C. just called, loves Suniti's *Goja*. Sees everything, of course. And I love the irony and humor in Monique's book.[23] Her unmistakable voice. In which she speaks deep truths. What she said about the absolute necessity of flattering men to get their attention reminds me of *The Box Closet*[24] (where Mother advises me?) *Lily Briscoe*[25] too? I say the same thing. The opening gambit, fawning attention, is in every commercial, in all the sinuous weaving (like Lily) of women's bodies, the bending of wrists, the placing of heads on hands, upturned faces and seductive little smile. Man: seductive indifference. As rigorous a training for this as for the Tea Ceremony. Or ballet (the correctly bent wrist) ... Today—eyes burn, limbs heavy as if each part of me is drooping with sleepiness. But yesterday wasn't particularly tiring. Not tiring enough? O lovely rain.

MAY 25. Yesterday Ann mailed my Royal Vic journal page to Steve.[26] Immediately, everything that was wrong with it sprang to mind. It was hard to read, too pale, mistakes wouldn't make him laugh ... The process of draining everything of pleasure. Immediate process like cutting a pig's (sheep's etc.) throat ... A calm sunny cool day ... Last night watched John McEnroe on A&E. Graceful as a cheetah with long flexible limbs flexing and twisting. He was doing this as a little boy. Impossible retrievals at the net, too fast for me to see. And now he's one of three umpires sitting above the court—infallible.

J. and her surprise that V. knows how to do therapy. Afterwards I thought of saying "Why not, it's not like training to be a shamaness." People's images of other people—over-simplified, shrunken. Even David S. did this—fitted

23. Monique Bosco, Québécoise writer.
24. *Lily Briscoe: A Self-Portrait*, Mary's first book, published by Talonbooks in 1981.
25. Mary's memoir based on her parents' letters and diaries, *The Box Closet*, was published by Talonbooks in 1987.
26. Stephen Osborne, editor of *Geist*.

people into a pre-conceived pattern: the rich person, the successful person, the person who went to Princeton, etc. ... Monique B.'s books—carefully, tightly woven as a weaverbird's nest but airy too, punctuation, paragraphs. M.C.'s structure makes its own time, a kind of expanded present, whereas Monique's is the strange timelessness of thought ... It does not pass, it's there held in suspension. It is memory, the time that arrests time and holds it motionless.

MAY 26. Cloudy, working up to rain? ...

In daily life—insignificant resentments; I feel Mother pulling my strings. The beautiful calm of Verena. Everything magically gets done including meals. Innumerable plants are planted, bushes pruned, etc. The lilac has reached its full glory, I think.

MAY 27, SUNDAY. Silence reigns in the house. Outside the slow changes of light to almost sunshine which darkens again & now a soft breeze moving leaves. Verena's plants prospering ... Looking through the piles of folders & envelopes I found writing I'd forgotten about just before the stroke that rejoiced my heart. Alive! ... The notes about waiting on the old iron bridge. And I think that the freewriting is my present way of releasing this inventive part of my mind, torpid but still active ... Monique's book[27] at breakfast about old age so exactly coincided with my own views that I laughed out loud. Examples cited of people who've lived to the age of 95, etc., with the implication that now we can follow their example, that it's easy, so-and-so plays golf, walks a mile a day ... Or the following dialogue: *"Comment vas-tu."* *"O.K."* *"Pas mieux que ça?"* The only acceptable answer is *"Très bien, merci."* I remember Father and his attempt at cheerfulness, "Pretty well." How could he possibly say, "Fine, thank you," when he knew that he was dying? The mordant humor of *Wit*.

MAY 29. Windy, sun coming out! Cool (12° C.) Heavy state. Drank a thimbleful (Cynthia's term) of the Balvenie. Too much! ... Betty Jean yesterday. What a surprise, round head, round body, dressed in black, looked almost like a tuxedo, seemed to be talking immediately with Alma about being a lesbian. Which made me feel completely at ease with her. A non-stop talker, seems to be pre-determined to have lunch here. She asked me 1000 questions about Eliz. Bishop, got out Gary Fountain & read what I said

27. Monique Bosco, *Méa Culpa*, Montreal: Hurtubise, 2001.

about her. (Good, to my surprise, and a lot of it.) Listened hungrily while I talked rashly about Bobbie,[28] M.C. and me, gave her *The Medusa Head*[29] (she went to Androgyny & got the others) talked about Elizabeth, M.C. and me and our meetings ... Meantime I was getting desperately tired, afraid she'd stay all afternoon, preparing speeches. "I'm afraid I've worn you out," she said at one point, but didn't leave space for an answer. Reminds me now of M.C.'s books, though you can climb out and re-enter, but there is something similar about the way one part is linked to the other, an overlapping device that locks the whole into a seamless sentence. The result—sublime in M.C.'s case and maddening in the cases of B.J., R.B., ... etc., etc. ... Exchanged warm hugs both with Elizabeth and B.J.—regardless of sexual orientation.

June 4. Another cold cloudy day. Ann yesterday. I can't find my old check, M.C.'s check. She hunts, doesn't find them, sits, says, "You *couldn't* have lost anything so important." I feel sick, on the verge of tears. She hunts in new filing box, finds everything ... I should have pointed out that this is the worst thing you can say to a person with memory loss. The point is that you *can* forget *anything*, important or not, and it's frightening ... Am I holding my own? Sometimes I think cutting Serax in half has helped. *Must start cutting half in 2.*

The sky—a prolonged sulkiness, a listless tossing-about of leaves but everything getting greener, standing straighter (the new delphinium). Wild morning-glory shaking everywhere.

June 21. Pale blue gentle cool day. Lily curved with her nose between her paws over my writing space. Dream. *I'm looking at a forested landscape—leaves on trees just budding—pink, grey. Above and behind them—the tops of dead pine trees sticking up.* "The pines are all dead!" I say. This morning it occurs to me that these are our dead friends and family. There are more dead ones all the time ...

Lovely feeling yesterday of directing garden activities, sawdust and mahogany chips as mulch. Moving birdstone down to little fountain garden, moving rabbit back. A nice sense of designing and Vogel doing all the work with lovely patience. Decisions about color of pebbles.

28. Barbara Deming, writer, activist, Mary Meigs' longtime partner.
29. Mary's second book, *The Medusa Head*, published by Talonbooks in 1983.

JUNE 24. ... My feeling of extreme slowness, of pushing and pulling a darning needle through sailcloth—my mind. Banal answers. Have you seen? Heard? Any birds? I've heard twitterings. Nestings. A deaf person believes no birds are there. Can't see them either. But—just now—Cynthia called, had seen a cardinal in her garden ...

Yesterday Verena got a beautiful dark blue, white-lined bowl at Rona & some polished stones, bigger than pebbles & we moved Feng Shui into it—much better but still something to doubt. Are they too shiny? Bigger stones (Newf) have been banished. Bowl much better ... Verena brought down my last complicated bone & wood sculpture for the bathroom, is going to make feet for the shingle woman in the blue hat. Real pleasure of looking at these things. And pleasure of writing. Out the window: foreground—green leading up to the gently bubbling fountain. Behind it the pale blue tightly clustered shaft of the delphinium, behind that a little apricot sun floating in dark green leaves ... Lily, her right paw doubled parallel to long hair on chest, head thoughtfully bent, fine white whiskers 4 1/2 inches long, stretches out paw, licks it now hidden under outstretched head on edge of notebook.

JUNE 28. Days have gone by. Roz has come, yesterday. Vogel & M.C. to Sims Rd. till today. Till late today? Terrible sourness of spirit à la Hopkins, jealousy, Vogel's ecstatic message picked up this morning. I wished that it would rain hard for 24 hours, that it would show its dreary side, but no, not a drop. And the horrible feeling of being a cranky, demanding old woman ...

Last night after supper I puttered laboriously around the porch putting the plastic cover on the table, dragging the dining-room chair inside, throwing the pillows on the kitchen floor (they had to be picked up by me, of course). This morning the silver tray from the dishwasher tipped over & all the knives, forks, spoons, had to be picked up off the floor with reacher—a dull desperation.

JULY 2. The spongy feeling in my head (last night horrid pain in left leg). Miky wedged himself between my upper half & the edge of the bed, he has staked out this space because Lily has conquered the lefthand lower corner. Warm and still for once, his whole length like a little bolster. Lily encroaching on my space now again, her paws on the magnifying glass fitting its curve.

JULY 6. Cool, cloudy, windy. Three peach-colored roses floating against dark green. Stone garden, scarlet geraniums, tiger lilies. I never get tired of these bits of changing color from this window and from the porch the clematis luxuriating over Sandy's star, the gate & Vogel's statue, bright orange still ... My eyes burn from the drops yesterday. This morning reading all Dr. C.'s instructions with nervousness—complications of pre and post-op instructions.[30] Dream, several days ago. *A vivid view like a bright colored photo—a beach scene between trees. A brown & black bear (brown nose) is standing. In another scene two of these bears (the cubs?) are curled comfortably together.* Next day I see a photo of black bears in *Canadian Wildlife* as endangered species.

JULY 13. An eternity seems to have gone by. A new life with Kat. Admirable, precise, not penetrable, no idea what she thinks of me, has an urgent need to explain things to me, to everybody? Doesn't mean she thinks I'm slow-witted? Vogel, too, the explanation, the contradiction, nothing I said was ever heartily agreed with. Was her mother like this? Or is it because I'm 84 years old? ... Is it my fault that so many people want to boss me? Is there some kind of psychological trap I set—uncertainty, etc.? I certainly seem to make myself so plain that I regret it or am locked into something, or not plain enough. "You said you didn't want yogurt for breakfast. You said you didn't like Minestrone," (true of Commensal). I said I was used to making instant decisions for myself, that I couldn't *always* decide (always know), had to think. What a luxury to be able to change one's mind in peace. To like something today & be disgusted by it tomorrow. Changes of mind are hard on the caretaker. Last night I dreamt that a mouse (grey) fastened its jaws on my hand. I shook it off, woke up.

JULY 15. Sunny with small snowy clouds. Mike has vanished again and I'm worried. He came in (or up?) and just ate a little breakfast. Lily in front of me, her right paw doubled up. My slightly dotty, wobbly state but worked 2 hours on *Goja*[31]—almost straightened out. "We're all slowly dying," says Suniti. This ties us together. Her voice, musical and melancholy and deep, is so real to me ... The perfect fully open pink clematis blossom this morning— on the porch side. Am I the only one to say clèmătis, not clemātis?

JULY 21. Another in a series of glorious hot days. My eyesight bad, a little better with reading glasses. Fell asleep 6:25 and could hardly walk when I

30. Mary was scheduled for a cataract operation in the fall.
31. Suniti's autobiography—Mary was writing a review.

woke up. Persistent blurriness but strange intensity of color, particularly blue. Rugs look freshly washed.

Sarah died July 21, 1998. Thornie July 2000.

July 22, Sunday. Windy, hot—somewhat pale sunshine. State of blurry eyes, slight nausea, wobbliness & discomfort. A violent wish to rub my right eye ... A craving, perhaps like the craving of a pregnant woman, for a hard-boiled egg. Indescribable texture of well-boiled yolk, dry, not rough, not smooth (the delicious egg-fruit from the great orchard Sally & Portia & I went to, with bright yellow yolk-like flesh). The immaculate polished white of the hard-boiled egg, combined with the yolk, with pepper & salt, a picnic. I can taste & smell it, the yolk crumbles, I pick up every crumb—delicately. A new scenario—the vision of a hard-boiled egg from a free-ranging hen, with a bright yellow yolk. I have had a stroke & can't talk. "Ah, bo-eh," I say urgently. Nobody understands. Can I laugh? In reality, so much is left and yet I can't fill in the blank pages of my agenda—Fri. and Sat. of this week—or remember who telephoned ...

July 23, Monday. My whole being blurry. A dread of measured explanation ... I'm dying to talk about control, its vices and devises and disguises and iron maidens and checkmates, how it can start as the most irresistible flattery and you see the fingers of an aye-aye hooking around a single hair of your head and delicately, affectionately prying it out and anchoring it. "I have never tried to control anybody in my life," says the aye-aye who does not admire an oyster's crude ways.

July 24. In the viscous medium. From my window so beautiful: big pale lavender hosta blossoms against dark green, and a full-blown pink rose beyond against almost black shade & viridian leaves ... K. says 3 clematis flowers on porch & vivid orange nasturtiums at edge of house. Lovely mingling of stones, blue top of post.

July 27, Saturday. My point of view has changed, the paranoia has faded. Useful explanations, mistaken interpretations. But the feeling like Iris Murdoch's that no human beings can ever understand each other, that they will make fatal mistakes of understanding, fatal summaries of character, mostly for the worse. A tendency to think the worst, a wish to misunderstand?

JULY 31, TUESDAY. August pushing softly like Lily with her hard head blotting out my work-space. Doesn't seem to move. Every day begins the same—cool, bright, blue, still. A few more pink clematis have opened on the porch railing. These lovely outward signs should make me happy—and the little vase of nasturtiums, a tiny daisy, perfect clematis, a continuum of all the bouquets in my summers like a bright chain. A kind of listless stirring of prey in a spider's web. I stare at the garden and now the glad blue gateposts have coincided with some old image in my head. The locking into place of the blue gate at Sims Road, an emotional & nostalgic locking as well as the almost-aphrodisiac of blue. And also a locking of something I made (the gate from an old window & a piece of decorative cast iron & old hinges ...).

Sally just appeared with Starhawk's e-mail about the Genoa protest, Fascist response, beatings, torture, arrests. The killing of a demonstrator, live ammunition. And I feel sick. Sally wants me to help compose an e-mail in response. That it's happening all over again. That the massive clot of hate is always there, has been growing waiting for a host and now this, seemingly harmless, unarmed, hard to define. Who are they? The innocent enemy. Will it be a war between good & evil again?

AUGUST 2, THURSDAY. The furry wall of Lily's back in front of me, a black stripe between white-tipped beige hairs on her side. A new position taking up strategic space. Is her tail less sumptuous? Was that a piece of it on the porch? Was my Lily worsted in the awful catfight? My scenarios go on and on & somebody always gets blamed: Eliz.—for having knocked the antler off the deer, for having jammed the lever on my Olivetti, etc. ... Collapse today after a good night's sleep. *Another dream about a shabby room full of shabby things (my room). I'm leaving it, carefully assembling & tidying the things as if it's important for each to remain in exactly that place.* This happens in my life now, my wish for nothing to change its position on this table. Sacrilege! My piece on *Goja*. Ridiculous effort to hide *Aimée & Jaguar*. So I cover it with the bag of Dolgo apples. This morning it's on top of the next pile of books & the apples are on top of Leonard & Trekkie's *Love Letters*.[32] Self-analysis shows it's my distaste for the nude photo on the cover of *A&J*. Kissing. Have I changed from 60 years ago?

AUGUST 4. Little alarms: the black cat dashes across my garden; yesterday's scab fell off dubious scaly patch near my ear, Dr. D. away till August 6th.

32. Judith Adamson, *Love Letters: Leonard Woolf & Trekkie Ritchie Parsons 1941–1968*, Plimico: 2002.

Everything seems shifting & uncertain in August. People repeatedly go—to Cape Cod, to Edmonton, to Maine, to Florida, come back and go somewhere else. I can never remember where or for how long; Verena, Lise, Cynthia, Martine & Myriam, Ann & Maureen. M.C. seems the most stable. The way I used to be—almost free ... Tobie[33] yesterday—her beautiful photos of her calligraphy, talks of the Morandi and Vermeer shows in London, her enthusiasm about my stone garden as if it had succeeded—the gate from one garden to the next mysterious shaky one, the stones and little fountain, the distant white bench under the Dolgo apple covered with small bunches of scarlet fruit. She made up the correct meanings.

MONDAY, AUGUST 6. A horrible dream woke me up at 5:30, my heart racing. *I was on a train platform. Arthur came along in a formal grey suit & hat (?). Cheerful. He pulled a black revolver out of his side pants pocket. It was shiny with square corners. He smiled, then put it back in the pocket again with some difficulty.* This seemed to me to be about death. A. showing me the way?

AUGUST 7. *Shame is a rusty edge* (Anne Carson).[34] Must I refuse the temptation to pick everything apart? Shame for me is not a rusty sharpness, not a dull clarity, is not the orange-brown jaggedness but formal edge of Sandy's iron star the beautiful metamorphosis merging iron with light with humidity, it is closer to mold, to an abominable smell that can be recalled in the middle of the night, that suffuses the body with burning heat, mounts steadily to the crown of the head. I know about shame that it is more like poisonous burning gas than a rusty edge. It can outlive the life-span of plutonium. It will outlive memory. It can't be stepped on in a cow pasture. Lockjaw doesn't impress it. It enters the souls of animals.

AUGUST 8. Dream. *I'm in a car, Sarah is driving. Or I'm seeing her driving, on a dirt road. She comes to a place where the bank of earth under the road is worn away. (She's driving on the right side of the road and of the car.) She keeps on going with her left wheels just clinging to the rim of the road and the right wheels over space, the car flat against the void. In the rest of the dream Sarah & Mother are interchangeable (this has happened in other dreams).*

My eyes prickle. Looking down at Bean's catalogue: rt. eye, clear & bright-colored cover; left eye—blurry, dull color, tinged with yellow grey.

33. Tobie Steinhouse, painter and friend
34. This was a freewrite (see page 135). Mary re-recorded it in her journal.

AUGUST 10. Dream. *I'm looking out at a muddy, choppy sea. Rain is falling, a grey curtain of drops. Later I wake up, want to pee. Start to get up, look for my shoes, not there & have a terrible time swinging around to get out of bed. Eliz. isn't in the chair. The mattress is spread out on the floor & I couldn't have gotten past it. Eliz. has stood up & is standing up with my shoes on.*

"The heart alone is what holds us here," B.W.[35] No other other.

AUGUST 11, SUNDAY. A feeling of complete inert blah. Yesterday Joanna announced that Lily was drooling abnormally upstairs & lying tautly & I thought of Lulu, Pirtty, Abychien. I brought her down & put her on my bed. Later in the afternoon she stopped drooling & seemed better, drank a tiny bit, lay down on a towel on my bed; last night lay on the cover near my left foot. Telephonings right & left, got # of 24-hr. vet for weekends, perhaps 2 hr. wait, on TransCanada. Decided to leave her in peace (Sally & I). She went out with Mike, was under the lilac & has now disappeared.

AUGUST 14. Yesterday, August 13, Lily was put to sleep. She cried when Sally came and tried to get up. Legs splayed out. Ann said she submitted quietly to being put in her cage but struggled & cried in the old way once she was in. Perfectly quiet when she got the shot. When Sally brought her home in the blue & white pillowcase & a green garbage bag she moved her a little and I thought she was still alive. Her eyes were a little open & seemed to be looking out; she was limp. A strange sourish smell. I touched her head, the short hairs on her forehead I'd studied so often—how they changed direction at the bridge of her nose. Sally dug a big hole below the back window after  carefully arranging her in her pillowcase, shovelled in dry earth, put a heavy smooth slate from the mine on top & Frances' half-finished little grey lamb on the slate & Lily's blue plastic bowl. She was wearing her green collar & ID bell and the silver cat Nihal had made about 3/4 inch high. My whole body aches with longing to see her stretched over a big area of my work-space with one paw stretched out. My Lily, who bonded with me in the course of the years and became my shadow. I could see her shadow passing under the bottom of the bathroom door or a black paw pushing its way about

35. Betsy Warland, poet, old friend. Mary is quoting from her latest book of poems *What Holds Us Here* (Ottawa: Buschek Books, 1998)—though in fact she has melded phrases from two different poems. "the heart alone / assures of an afterlife" and "oxygen / … is what holds us here."

1/2 inch under. Her chubby paws, wide furry chest resting on their wide support. Her anxious slightly petulant expression and glorious eyes. On my lap she turned her head sideways & pushed it hard against my stomach. Or lay spread out on me when I took my nap after treading uncomfortably. She could run like the wind at Sims Road and race part way up one of the maple trees. Her almost roundness was a comical joy—and her serious & severe look. Also quite alarming when enraged. A quiet purr & so loving settling in such loving acceptance in my lap.

AUGUST 18. Miky has taken over my entire work-space so I'm writing in the notebook on my lap. There's no way to get him off without spilling an avalanche of papers on the floor.

MIKE

Eyes bad today. Glasses inadequate. Depression because 2 more months of this before operation (Oct. 17). Long fax from Suniti at 7:30 AM. So welcome—most sensitive response, she said; suggested small changes which she can make ...

AUGUST 21. ... Feel wobbly & apprehensive & am plagued by threat of mild diarrhea. No sense of humor. Red-faced bumbling Dr. Y. Mike is very remote today, out most of the night. Lise's comforting talk on the phone last night. And Davy[36] came back after 3 days perfectly alright.

AUGUST 23. Subdued light as if there were an eclipse of the moon. And a wobbling in my mind, eyesight bad. A linking of omens. Verena's D.,[37]

36. Lise's cat.
37. "D." is Mary's abbreviation for "diarrhea."

Pierrette's terrible stomachache that doubles her up with pain. The poisoning of the earth and air and water. In the QSPB report sightings of barn swallows dropped from 25 (not many!) to 0 in 1 year. Only 1 bobolink. But a bumper year for 2001 at Point Pelée. Birds dropped from the sky, some literally fell. Judy's report of huge flocks of grackles. Fallada the horse[38] whose head was cut off & mounted on a blue post, who spoke wise words.

AUGUST 26, SUNDAY. Rain and thunderstorms predicted but seem impossible, a cool overcast day. My cautionary trips every few minutes to the bathroom, just as well, too. Eyes very blurry. I'm heartened by the prospect of glasses & afraid they won't help much. Sylvie so ready to be nervous about doing things badly & does everything well. Silences. My fear of being indiscreet ... With Suzanne more comfortable silences. Finding things—the perennial problem and now it's the doll closet painting. The exact moment when one puts something somewhere. I sent Sylvie on a wild goose chase in the basement. My theory about eclipses, the sense that most of another person is always in eclipse ... (the most common mistake, to feel responsible for the unknown).

AUGUST 31. Called M.C. and she was laughing merrily & happily and her happiness was genuine. Her eye is much better, sees clearly near and far. My huge feeling of relief. There is blood in her eye but this will go away. I don't remember having this. Today my eye hurts in spite of the new lens. Perhaps I overworked it. As usual have to keep running (this is a slight decrease in slowness) to the bathroom. Muggy breathless air, mild sunshine. Judy's[39] pale yellow straight hair, black and white striped long-sleeved T-shirt. A red squirrel found a way of getting to all the food she'd left for the birds and had devoured it and she turned the hose on it—a strong blast. This is the sort of thing I would have done once—Now? All my thinking about teaching animals a lesson has been gradually changing. Judy was driven berserk by a woodpecker who came and drummed with his bill on her metal roof to serenade her (my theory) by banging on it herself—so loudly that he never came back. Was he serenading her or laying claim to the roof? Anyway, the story made my heart ache for the woodpecker. Too close to my own kind of retaliation? The see-sawing of hardheartedness and compassion.

38. A horse's head mounted on a gatepost in Mary's garden was named after Fallada the talking horse in Grimms' fairy tale "The Goose Girl," whose head is nailed to a gate. (See photo on page 128.)
39. Judy Adamson, writer, old friend and one-time neighbor.

SEPTEMBER 1. Gail last night and her marvellous red hair, the tightest curls, which she unbound at one point to show it to me like a sunburst from her head ... A wonderful pair, she and Suzanne who is like a very tall graceful Greek athlete & dancer, every movement graceful. We had such fun yesterday with the book of conjugations. Forgotten verbs and tenses popped into my head. And French tenses are amazing and funny, *asses* & *eusses* & *fusses* in the subjunctive. S.'s broad culture a real joy ...

SEPTEMBER 3. Labour Day. Isabel last night. I thought she'd been coached by Leonie but no, she hadn't spoken to her ... This morning she emptied the dishwasher, a bit vague about helping me get dressed. Cursory washing. Wanted to brush my hair. Evidently surprised when I didn't do things the way every normal woman does. Last night: "You had a hair wash. Who did it?" ... "Sylvie," I say. "Your hair needs to be washed," she says in her flat, slightly peremptory voice. A discussion about "nursing." My question, "Have you had any nursing experience?" She thought I meant breast feeding and said no. She had never married or had children. I said I hadn't either. "You never had boy friends?" "Oh yes, sure boy friends." My persistent craven dishonesty. Fear that she'll trot out the story of Sodom and Gomorrah. She sat down at the kitchen table. "Do you believe in God?" She'd begun by a question like, "Have you given your life to Jesus?" Which I'd half-heard and answered by saying that I had slight diarrhea every morning after breakfast. "Do you believe in God?" she said firmly (sternly). I tried to explain about an omnipotent life force that's in all creation including animals & plants—part of the genome. "Are you a scientist?" "No, but I read scientific articles."

SEPTEMBER 4, TUESDAY. A soft dampish day, still drops on the window. The two full-blown pink roses growing paler. Yesterday a strong sense of the garden's beauty as I stumbled cautiously around. Intensely orange nasturtium and their big flat leaves like water-lilies lying on air instead of water but very thin, a vivid green. They are flourishing in spite of drought. Tiny daisies 1/4 inch diameter. Bright yellow flowers the color of dandelions but the shape of gerberas—tight-packed petals and small centers. Sylvie rearranged the lavender branches & dug around it to loosen the soil and found a little spray of lavender. She knows the Latin names of some of the flowers, she touches the plants with the tenderness of a true gardener.

Dreams: *1) In a fancy patisserie like Le Gascogne. I buy some cut-up peaches that look very good. Then walk on & come to some that look even better and want to buy some. The colors are extraordinary—very yellow with their red and yellow skins on. An altercation with the woman at the counter; she dawdles around and never does sell them to me. This time too, I want to pee. (The woman is wearing a white apron.) 2) I'm standing (dressed) at the edge of a beach running along the ocean which is an extraordinary joyful blue—the color of reef water (cerulean). People are swimming, their heads bobbing about.* There is no surf but when I wake up I'm reminded of the beach on the Pacific near the Heads where I went with Ruth, Marj, Jude and Jane to Marj's house. The waves were breaking and rolling in, lorikeets, and king parrots, a strong wind, the four laughing friends with their arms around each other, their legs planted firmly, while I sat further back on the beach, fully dressed. The ocean was more ultramarine than in my dream but the feeling of joy and lightness of heart were the same—and the great breadth of the ocean. These were the first dreams in full color I've had for a long time—as bright as the colors I see with my right eye now.

Reality or the instant scenario, the nightmare equivalent which is supposed to prepare me for the worst? M.C. didn't come yesterday. Dire reasons spring to my mind. Possible disasters—death, sickness, M.C.'s eye again, Michèle. The reason—that she didn't say she was coming yesterday but today—isn't admitted. Because it accuses me of forgetfulness? Of not writing it down.

SEPTEMBER 8. Pure joy when I see the pale sheet of rain & hear thunder—like the sound outside the apartment house when boards are being thrown down the chute outside. Not predicted. My ears now make strange distortions. Last night I put on the Schubert CD L. & S. gave me & it was the piano quartet (2nd movement) in *The C. of S.*—such nostalgia—during the sudden soft rainfall when Cissie and I are looking out, she is standing in the doorway & I'm at the window—a long pensive look, much emphasis on white hair, sentimental in a nice way. The extraordinary beauty of the Schubert. But presto movement sounds all wrong because my ears screen out certain sounds & admit others. I'm thinking of getting a small portable CD player like M.C.'s with earphones.

SEPTEMBER 9. Dream. *I'm the pilot of a big plane like a 747 and bring it in smoothly—I'm the only person on it. I get out by walking down aluminum (steel?) steps, swinging down with my arms and then jumping lightly to the ground. I'm holding a folded section of newspaper in one hand to throw away. A white-bearded man comes up the steps to help me, a stout and pleasant face ... I say I don't need help, thanks, and wake up.* This dream is full of self-sufficiency—specially the easy jump down to the runway; I'm wearing lightweight canvas sneakers. All evening I'd had a delightfully sexy feeling, the first for months (since my strokes?) and touched my responsive breasts & thought maybe I could work up very slowly to orgasm. I remembered one post-stroke time when this came to nothing except exhaustion—a warning, I thought, because my heart was beating hard & I'm ever-afraid of having another stroke.

SEPTEMBER 14. Almost a week has gone by since I last wrote. Another? I've said nothing about Sept. 11, the terrorist attack. The crumbling towers & flames, the Pentagon, the people flinging themselves out of the towers before they fell, the chaos and continuous horror and clean-up & retrieval (for DNA) of the tiniest body parts, the pall of smoke still over New York & dust & tiny pieces of paper like snow. Preparations for war with Afghanistan, the Taliban, the calling up of reserves, Bush & strategy for revenge. Clinton goes to funeral for firefighter captain. Over 300 firefighters killed. People with rage in their hearts beat up any Muslim at hand ... Cynthia called last night—lovely—coming Monday. D. began at 5 this morning, and at intervals, and hovering now. The fine trembling high blood pressure? I repeat & repeat "Be still," etc.—to no avail.

SEPTEMBER 16, SUNDAY. Sylvie, a shampoo, morale-boosting, M.C.'s surprising fax from Key West. Total collapse. Jovette called and Maureen,[40] & I called Mike and we talked at length. She wants to understand the presence of evil in the world, says she *has* to understand. I said it was seen as good by the people who believed they were immediately admitted into God's kingdom. Much harder for me to understand are the grisly murders, torture, rape, etc. done to children. To what extent do we have to "understand"? Words are incapable of explaining—glib and superficial, it is what will be forever unknown, why *cogito, ergo sum*? We don't have to think to be. We've been given something so inadequate, not up to the great task, and expected to figure out the problem of good and evil. Naturally the solution would be for a bully to rough up a Muslim woman doctor in the elevator at the Royal Vic—or to fly an American flag. Or to intone the slogan of the American West—"Dead or Alive!" My mind like a wet string mop. And time is moving so slowly. I crawled from 5 AM to 6:30, grudging light, it seemed, through blue drawn curtains. Suzanne coming soon, she & Claire know each other.

40. Maureen Brady, writer and old friend.

SEPTEMBER 27, WEDNESDAY. A beautiful cool day. The new pink rose, full-bloom, is floating against the dark shade at the back of the garden, high on its stem. A yellow one on the east side. "The little grace of every day"—there are lots of them. I want to save the images of the roses for winter. And Fallada with her nose pressed against her neck. She seems to be looking gravely, modestly up. She seems to be turning grey—a kind of rust? Almost two weeks have gone by without my writing in my journal ... Miraculous sensibility of animals. When I'd hurt Lily's feelings by paying too much attention to Miky I felt I had to beg her forgiveness. Her reproachful face.

SEPTEMBER 28. A horrid cold & I feel awful. Never enough Kleenex and a cough that almost turned into a fit of throwing up (but not quite), groaning the while. Finishing up *Passionate Friends*.[41] Miles has the instinct for the exactly right word, the shape of it, in prose, and seems to find it in Fullerton's poetry. At first her use of sentimental words like "methinks" or "wost" can be held against her but the feeling is always authentic, in fact, M.F. seems transparently honest and if she could hide under the shelter of anonymity it was because people were deliberately blind then, so determined not to apply the word lesbian to two women that they didn't look at the evidence. Some tower of belief would come toppling down. Do I have any towers of belief left? In the genetic truth of violence? Does it mean something important to me, like the gratuitous violence I've sometimes seen in myself, just from being in a bitchy mood? What does Blake think— *The Poison Tree?*

Shapes are moving across my field of vision, my eyes prickle. A fit of coughing. Suzanne says all this discharge of mucus shows how much we are a part of the earth's matter ... Gloria's black cat wandering around & finding a new place for a cat toilet. Mike has changed his schedule and goes out for the morning, lies on G.'s porch & doesn't come on my table anymore. I've given up ... S. so much like a tall slim Greek athlete with easy & graceful bearing comes into the room silently on her white feet like hinges opening small pendulum movements of her arms. Like a clock-figure, in fact, moving across the quiet space of the dining room.

OCTOBER 3, WEDNESDAY. Out of focus still. The body and mind and eyes. This morning dawn seemed to go on forever. When I woke up it was already a little light and my watch said 4-something & I thought it was broken. Got

41. *Passionate Friends: Mary Fullerton, Mabel Singleton, and Miles Franklin*, by Sylvia Martin (London: Only Women Press, 2001).

E. up repeatedly finally to hobble to the bathroom. By then it was 5:30. I finished *Passionate Friends* and read a little *Prévert* and F. Kahlo & felt able to see in them both what I hadn't seen the first time: *Prévert* a kind of perfect grace, weightless language contains meaning without the substance of language. The meaning closer to an image—Napoleon? Who has added that handwritten last line? I seem to go to understanding through resistance. Kahlo: her physical appearance, turbulent passions & orderly handwriting. Her love for that huge mass of life, Rivera. Her dramatization & mythification of herself—the wounded bird, the archangel (I must read Fuentes' introduction) and her perfectly legible round words. Is this from her will to control her words in her shattered state—but complete freedom of images? Leaden literal heaviness of book.

OCTOBER 6. An infinitely long night, woke up first 2-something, dawn lightness, it seems, in the room—dragged on quite comfortably, finally got up 6:45, having to pee. Rain, & now, it seems, a slow clearing, waving of leaves, the inner light that isn't sunlight. On the street side bright yellow fallen leaves on the pavement through the scrim of the lace curtain look exactly like dappled sunlight ... My black pants seem to be about to fall off. The thin tape can't be pulled tight enough—a problem for Sylvie. Limpness, cough churning, cold holding its own. Loretta's wonderful sense of order, soothing, disposes of everything with a kind of divine justice. A scarlet geranium & a last nasturtium leaning out from the window box.

OCTOBER 8. Cold. 1° this morning, wind & sun. Two rosebuds waving in the wind. Scarlet geranium still O.K. & flowers in windowbox. Zinnias? I'm waiting for Suzanne ... I've been falling asleep, toppling over almost, the mysterious state of collapse. The Third World War, scary & depressing, can reach everywhere. Those "dead" relentless eyes, not icy nor steely but unflinching? Pitiless, do not seem to blink, unsmiling mouths—so a photograph of two Taliban men at ease & smiling, surprised me. Just with each other. Story of doctor who'd helped a brother and sister together and was beaten up by the Taliban.

Yesterday: M.C., Michel, Gabrielle, Claudine with the Sims Road video and a bounty of eggs, a big butternut squash, perfect red onions, tomatoes, all organically grown ...

OCTOBER 15. Collapse again & still. At breakfast read *Nightwood*. Robin's desertion of Nora. Haunting images, Gothic but always accurate even when crazily inspired like Robin's smile like the grim smile of someone on whom a bird has just obeyed a natural law ... Djuna Barnes' humor is part of her writer's anatomy. I think of Irma's mother, Polly, sitting in Washington Square on a bench with Djuna Barnes and chewing the breeze. Irma described this to me. How it was a friendship that flourished on the bench. And they must have laughed together.

Golden apple leaves dancing & glinting in the sun. The pink rose seems suddenly to have bobbed up into view. It's another mild day and the garden is untouched by frost. Nasturtiums, snapdragon, cosmos in little vase. One splendid deep pink zinnia in ꙮ. Overwhelming sleepiness. A feeling of no bones or muscles.

OCTOBER 17. I woke up this morning with a feeling of wellness— comfortable, warm, energetic—that won't last, "dangerously well." Now, 3 PM, total collapse, bleary prickly eyes. A few efforted exercises after my nap. Suzanne is making corn bread in the kitchen ... *A dream last night about someone like Marie at CHUS.*[42] *She's explaining to me how she fell in love with someone who already had a lover. I listened in silence. Then, to reassure her, I said, "I can't say that I wouldn't have done the same thing myself."*—2 negatives, woke up and kept saying the phrase over to remember it ...

Yesterday the cataract op. Quite calm. Not Dr. Connally, a youngish man with dark eyes & hair. Everybody friendly & tenderly smiling before: "I'm Luta," "I'm Nancy," afterwards I wanted to say "Goodbye everybody! Thank you!" Nobody looked at me; another patient was being wheeled in.

OCTOBER 18. Cold, *windy*, bitter. I asked Dr. C. who'd done the operation and he said he'd done it. He said my dark-eyed man was probably a resident. And I remembered that yes, he had on a green gown, but obviously got screwed up again. Resident certainly there at end, told me coughing hadn't mattered, squeezed my arm nicely.

OCTOBER 19, FRIDAY. This morning I overslept, heard Eliz. call me, it was 6:50. Everything seemed clear & fresh & bright-colored; now, 5 pills and 3 eye-drops later and reading *Nightwood* at breakfast, my eyelids (both eyes) smart & vision is less precise. The yellow Dolgo leaf brilliant in the sun,

---

42. *Centre Hospitalier de l'Université de Sherbrooke.* Mary stayed there immediately after her stroke in 1999.

looks like a golden rose. The yellow leaves have almost all blown off. For some reason Suzanne couldn't see the leaf. She said that because of near-sightedness from childhood she's never been able to see clearly when she woke up in the morning.

OCTOBER 20. My eyes the same as yesterday—color wonderful but sharpness of vision (not that sharp to begin with) getting myopic as the morning wears on. And eyelids. Specially on right side! As if specks of dust were in eyes—discomfort (not pain) as they say, feeling of strain. Fall issue of *Geist* came and my RV journal page not there—a dull disappointment and at the same time a pretext for running myself down, though I see it wouldn't have been appropriate after Sept. 11—at least not yet.[43] And yet to be in that good company, since it's a fat special issue ...

2:38. The Dolgo leaves almost gone; a few golden patches left, and quiver of green leaves still in the wind. Intensely blue sky.

OCTOBER 24. Warmish—14 degrees and the turning up of light under fine overcast. Still the single scarlet geranium & 2 rather bedraggled nasturtiums in the windowbox visible only from my table ... My state of mind depends on who I'm talking to. With A., I feel pushed and hassled, she seems to flash pieces of paper under my nose—to sign, to think about. The idea of putting the inventory into some kind of order throws me into a panic—to check for mistakes, same bequest to 2 different people. Missing brain-cells, the memory cells. Necessary remembering like Cynthia's right of refusal (sounds wrong). Things I can't (and will never?) remember (like the names of the husbands of great nieces, Logan's father). Shameful neglect of birthdays, etc. always a hopeless situation. Suzanne told me that her mother—with beginning Alzheimer's—is pursued all day long by a woman with a more serious case, who forgets almost immediately when she is told not to do it (the pursuing). No way to solve this problem which drives Suzanne, her mother and the staff crazy. What would happen in a perfectly run institution with compassionate understanding, etc. S.'s standards are very high, I feel a dull despair when she talks about how people *should* be. Doctors don't take the time to connect with their patients. Dr. K. doesn't *have* to take so many patients, Dr. C. when he starts examining the wrong eye, is shockingly negligent. I realize that I've lost my sense of indignation, it dried up somewhere along the way (like estrogen) in my effort to keep calm. Why

43. Mary's piece, titled "Keystroke," appeared in the Spring 2002 issue of *Geist*.

does it matter as long as the eye ops are a success? True, Dr. C. couldn't care less and Dr. K. can't spend any time talking, though she *is* interested in my case. My mouth opens to explain why the salary of the medicare system makes it hard to live as comfortably as a U.S. doctor. True, no? But S. knows all this. I'm preternaturally sensitive to my own lame, hoarse explanations & defenses. And am weighed down by an awful heaviness, physical & mental. The feeling that Dr. B. won't want to take me on. No precise symptoms except fatigue & a runny nose & blurry eyes ...

On the subject of ideal doctors I talked about Wister who'd come here just to talk to me about the pain of shingles, asked me endless kindly pertinent questions, the ideal old-fashioned doctor who did have time for his patients—gentleness, real interest. Suggested the mantra, "Be still and let my peace enter you and give you strength." This has calmed me ever since— even this morning and every morning about 4–6 when my heart (whole body) seems to be emitting a fine whirring, a tenseness. This morning I couldn't get back to sleep again but felt relaxed ... Just remembered—the dream about the round table about 15 feet below calm sunlit water with children seated around it, dressed in luminous summer colors like the colors in Piero della Francesca. Had something to do with Wister.

OCTOBER 25, 10:20. Francine has just left. Said perhaps Coumadin dose is too low ... blood pressure 130/80. Groundless worries as usual; I'd imagined everything from Parkinson symptoms to Anthrax. What are they? Whatever they are I can imagine them. "And don't worry," said the kindly Francine, looking so sweetly dykish in a navy blue cable-knit sweater & black pants & sturdy flat brown leather shoes. Deep voice. Suzanne B, too, has a deep (melodious) voice ... It's dark outside, an agitated dance of yellow leaves. The flame-bush turns from a dull purplish as it loses the green in its leaves—to crimson at the top—working its way down. Yesterday I went slowly down and went around the garden. This is always a joy and yesterday specially so, the earth a rich almost black damp everywhere, nasturtiums (3?) hiding under the flat umbrellas of perfectly circular green leaves, everything flourishing in the round bed, no sign of a cat—2 snapdragons & little clumps of mottled dark leaves. A triumph for Verena. And among the clematis leaves a *single flower*, almost purple (or dark mauve) & 2 beautiful mauve flowers about 1 in. diameter quite tall & straight near Lily. Suzanne had picked the 2 pink rosebuds & today these have opened a little & are exquisite. There's still a yellow rosebud, 2 cosmoses & the faithful scarlet geranium. On the kitchen table: the pink roses, tiny dianthus (crimson). Garden: bright yellow-green of yew, blue-green of weeping spruce & juniper, the last.

OCTOBER 27. The roses growing bigger, perfect one grew to 7" x 7", petals stayed on to the end and then Loretta put it on Lily's grave. I still feel the pain of her loss when I look at her serious anxious face, her white whiskers and the white hairs sprouting from her ears the M on her forehead, printed just over her staring eyes. Black defining her nose. My Lily. Today the flame bush dull purple still at the top and yellow Dolgo leaves still bright but not golden. The vine on the fence opposite is a pebbled scarlet, crimson, pink, like a big rug draped over the top ...

Reading *Nightwood* at breakfast, I went through the usual jumps from exasperation to a keen delight. In Matthew's company Norah talks more and more like him; she's melodramatic & overblown and I want to say "for God's sweet sake, Norah, cool it." Which M. does say. In fact he is amazingly patient and compassionate and the whole scene is piercingly real, I think the next minute. My memories of the book were all wrong; I thought the doll took up much more space, I forgot that Robin had murdered it, I'd evidently skipped all the brilliant monologues of the doctor (also the scene where Norah goes to see him in his disgusting dirty & untidy room [he's] wearing women's clothes).

OCTOBER 31. Hallowe'en. Standard time ... Yesterday en route to Dr. K.'s, the bluest sky I've ever seen. My new lenses? Last night I was afraid of frost and asked Suzanne to cut the yellow rosebud and the zinnia. This morning the thermometer said -2°. The rosebud exquisite. The zinnia petals already a little touched by cold at the edges (pale) ... Dream: (last night) *I'm standing at a window like the ones facing west in my big studio and in the same way I look down and see stones I want to bring in. Each one has an inscribed symbol on its back that seems full of meaning. Then I see a calm lake at the bottom of the hill. There is a canoe sitting there quietly and a man in it slumped over at a right angle with his elbows like wings on the gunwales. I think he's dead and get up to tell somebody. But am still interested in retrieving the stones & try to memorize their exact position in the pile.* I used to do this at Sims Road. Always hard to find the ones that looked so enticing from the inside. Is this about my immobility?

The 2 pink roses holding on to life. The big one doesn't drop its petals but gets limper and as light as tissue paper, the smaller one with tight-held petals like a peony—a beautiful patience in each of them, they know how to age like very old Chinese women in paintings (or vice versa). The last cosmos has died less elegantly, crumpled.

NOVEMBER 2, FRIDAY. Rain stillness. Yellow leaves still generate light, trunks of Dolgo & maples charcoal black. Dr. S. hasn't called yet. Collapse, lethargy. A dream about Bobbie. *We are in a hotel room, young, familiar & happy. B is wearing light blue-grey pajamas, looks like the self I knew long ago. I don't remember what we talked about* ... My brain lumbering along as usual and writing doesn't coincide with its lively states. Miky, too, listless, lies on my bed all day & quietly near me at night. Only occasionally interested in my black shoelaces & other dangling objects that catch his eye—his staring yellow eyes ...

Yesterday Linda, Loretta's friend ... 59, tall & slim with blonde hair and a beautiful kind face with classical features. We got into a conversation about birds. There is a *"petit* one" who lived in a hole in a tree on the Mt. & would come out & sit motionless & invisible every day—not there this year. What a pang I felt at this ... At one point Linda gathered her things & seemed about to go & then folded up gracefully on the floor & chatted some more. Talking one of my most exhausting activities. Not to be dreary ...

M.C. yesterday. Is going to Belgium soon, something to do with the Academy. Seems fearless. Terrorist threats. Big suspension bridges in U.S. Why not just a decoy to divert attention from other targets? Meantime the Dow Jones & the Canadian markets are plummeting. Dr. S. doesn't call ... In one photo Lily's tail is fat & bushy, in the more recent one it is quite thin. Proof that a lot was pulled out by Gloria's black cat ... Almost noon, no call from Dr. S. Just read the piece about ecofeminism & Virginia Woolf—*The Waves, Flush*, etc. ... [44] Wonderful. I think about my own connection with "the real," i.e. our identity with the whole of creation, think about the usefulness of language to express it. I can still use words but don't have the energy to fly with them ... they're like sight & hearing—dimming—"a dimming down." Perhaps I never went deeply into thought but had bursts of word-energy (like the freewriting now—what is it? Lucky illuminations in a sort of embracing fog. A locking of meanings by accident). But if I want to answer the questions how far do you go? How do you act on it? I can only answer I feel a quiver of joy when I think of apparently simple organisms— worms, thrips with nervous systems that have evolved like ours, with identical genes.

---

44. "Writing the Real: Virginia Woolf and an Ecology of Language," by Elizabeth Waller, *Bucknell Review* Vol. XLIV, No. 1 (2000).

NOVEMBER 3, SATURDAY. I'm waiting for Dr. S. to call at 9. A mild day, windy, the flame tree bright (deep) pink-crowned in the sun. Yellow rose still in kitchen, pink ones giving up ...

Dr. S. said that the mild shocks Dr. D. will give me can help fatigue & maybe prevent another stroke. But I was scared anyway & called Marisa[45] who was very reassuring, said there was no reason to be scared ... M. very good-humored & kind these days & gives me courage, doesn't mind my calling at 9:15 on a Saturday morning ... My meticulous lists of medications & ailments useless, Dr. S. not interested, of course.

NOVEMBER 4, SUNDAY. Horribly sluggish & wobbly. I was waked up this morning at 4:30 by the long ring of an alarm clock—in my head. Leonie said no, no ringing, and went into an unintelligible account of a dream she'd had about her boyfriend. Her frustration when I can neither hear nor understand, comes close & more or less shouts ... People I can hear: Loretta, Joanna, Sylvie ... Suzanne when she doesn't shout. Can't hear: S. & L., M.C., Claire. (Drooling bad today.) The flame tree is indescribably beautiful, the red like the red in a worn Persian rug but not like it, not crimson, scarlet, vermilion ...

NOVEMBER 5. Limpness, fear of falling; seems to have become habitual. Worse after thyroid and blood sugar pills? I just drowsed off in my chair. Have trouble pushing pen ... Reread Wister's *Idle Hours* from 1932, aged 17. Really good, lucid, a big vocabulary and sense of humor. I remember my snide laughter and his fury when I found his piece about *Leda & the Swan*— Yeats, in the dusty attic at the Annex. How he pursued me and snatched it out of my hand. I remember innocent naiveté about what the swan was doing. But what did I know? Didn't I ask him what an orgasm was on the morning of his marriage? The superiority of his mind to mine, his marvellous memory and my snottiness. And now—instant forgetfulness (mine) and sluggishness of mind ... A sprinkling of bright raindrops on the window seem lopsided because of light as on a quarter moon on the lower left side. Different sizes. Dolgo apple almost bare of leaves, maple leaves a bright yellow green. One just flew down quite close. I must find a color that fits the wonder of the flame tree. The special treat of a frostless October? Does it last longer, this slow spectacle? ...

45. Marisa Zavalloni, college professor, old friend.

NOVEMBER 7. J.N.'s[46] new show opens—*Configurations*, it's called. The inability to cope. A leaf just seemed to jump from the tree with the impetuous movement of a bird. The flame tree more splendid than ever. The yellow rose still full-blown on the kitchen table ... I'm in my muddled state—chronic now. Last night my feet hurt, the spot on my ankle hurt, yesterday Dr. N. hurt, poking sharply in my ears for wax. First gruff & macho (thought I was too sure of myself?). Dr. N.: "What have you come here for?" M.: "Because I'm deaf and hope you can help me to hear better." Dr. N.: "Well, first I have to look and see if there's any wax in your ears, then I have to get it out, then I have to refer you to my assistant for a hearing test." I have a feeling that I'm talking to a large growling dog & become extremely humble. Fascinating how he becomes friendly, explains everything as he goes along. He gets a lot of wax out and it hurts. The sharp point of his instrument makes me cough, then sneeze & clench my fists (pain) but I hear better ...

NOVEMBER 8. The habitual feeling of swimming through resistant fluid, denser than water, though Dr. N.'s cleaning helped watery feeling in my head. A.'s telephone cut my message off again just at the crucial second, after my *politesses*, when I was about to explain why I'd called. I called back. Synonyms: wrath, ire, fury, irascibility, temper, impatience, rage, irked, irate. Annoyed, irritated, choleric, pissed off. There must be many more, not entirely appropriate ...

[Pierrette] brought me a Gascogne crème brulée in its beautiful white ramekin (same word in French). I said I'm not supposed to eat sugar. "Oh a little won't hurt you" in her most winsome tone. Suzanne & I tried it at supper—sublime, creamy, sugary, crunchy.

NOVEMBER 9. The yellow rose still holding up on the kitchen table. It has pointy petals, a head that never bends. Ineffable flame tree. Yellow-green leaves spin down on its mounded top. I hope it will last for Verena. Dreams. *I have wet the bed. I stand looking down on it—rumpled white sheets on double bed—with dull horror, think it can wait, and go off, leaving it wet. I'm going back to meet Miss Balfour in a restaurant.* About childhood wetting of bed? But Miss B.[47] friendly ... Some nice dreams, gently erotic. *I hold a woman's hand, I look into her eyes, we run lightly down a beach.* Lots of dreams about easy

---

46. Joanna Nash, artist, friend.
47. Miss Balfour was Mary's childhood nurse.

running or walking, about beautiful objects, fabrics, etc. The dream of looking down from a great height (a cliff) into the open, empty hull of a white schooner with a tall bare mast & no sail. The water is satiny pale blue ...

NOVEMBER 10, SATURDAY. The burst of deep pink-red of the flame tree and above it to the left bright yellow-green maple leaves at the back of Gloria's garden. Dolgo leaves almost blown away, brick wall visible again & house beyond—winter state but living & vivid still with autumn. The awful gloom of Sept. 11 superimposed over and in everything ... Reading Ursula LeGuin's Bryn Mawr commencement speech, ringingly feminist back then, impertinent and funny. She speaks for Everywoman, every woman's voice, activities, oneness with the earth, the language of babies and food (cooking) all excluded. Art, of course. Absurd defenses spring to mind. Why? Because this man's world was where I lived for so long, enjoying it? I've been through all this before and come into a calm place. That was where I found my voice and was accepted—an upper class rich woman—"rich" is as hard to say as "lesbian"—just as hard now, in fact lesbian is much easier now. I decided to write an update of *Lily Briscoe*.

The flame tree, the yellow rose, still holding on. The flame tree is a soft color, doesn't suggest blood or flag red, not aggressive or triumphant. It is comforting and warm like mohair, *"Insaisissable."* I luxuriate in trying to find words & can't even find an approximation. The flame tree color can't be called faded. It's *sui generis* ... I have a fainting feeling in every cell. Falling scenarios. If I lean sideways I have to make a special effort not to keep going like Sarah when I was with her.

NOVEMBER 11, SUNDAY. Remembrance Day. 2 degrees today but big yellow-green leaves still and flame tree and yellow rose, drying on its straight stem with quiet defiance. Nov. 15 is still the record (I must look for watercolor) ... Sept. 11, says Bin Laden, was "good terrorism." His message to the world— "good" means successful? Today—grudging movements of body. Horrid night from 3:45 to 6:00—spasms, ankle hurt, had to pee every half-hour ...

NOVEMBER 12. -4° C. this morning. The shadows of branches and a few blowing maple leaves on the brick wall today. Still a burst of flame lying on shadow. Yesterday Sylvie brought in 3 slender branches. Color ranging from pink to deep pink-red, and the last yellow rosebud which began to open. And she potted a geranium with two buds on it. She has a sure and delicate way with plants, which prosper for her, inside or out. Her panic when the colors on the L.L. Bean rug ran in her washing, though she'd predicted it & I'd said, "Oh no, it will be alright." She thought it was old & precious; hard to reassure her ...

NOVEMBER 13. Moving to the pivot on which every week swings. Tuesday— a comfortably long stretch of days, I think, no engagements and then— tipping of time, imbalance as if I were keeling over, unable to stop. When Eliz. asks me if I had a good weekend, if I saw lots of people I can't think of anybody I saw, anything I did. On Sunday Sylvie cut the yellow rosebud & some delicate flame tree branches with pink to pink-red leaves. The rosebud has opened into a small almost full-blown flower, the geranium she potted is flowering. The flame tree leaves are as beautiful as ever. She has an uncanny influence, some kind of prehistoric speech she was born speaking for reassuring plants. They stay green, they don't lose leaves, they flower ... When she's upset about something her mobile face screws itself up & reminds me of the language I invented for the Brown children for conversing with chimpanzees ...

Today one of those still, waiting days. Waiting for that 40% chance of rain? The possibility that the plane crash will be a terrorist act after all. This too is waiting, for terror or relief. A terrorist strategy ... Last night I amused myself by thinking of the huge spinster family of misses: Miss Treatment, Miss Carriage, Miss Step, Miss Information, Miss Pell, Miss Take, Mis-le-toe, Miss Behavior. On and on.

NOVEMBER 16, FRIDAY. Ms. Ogyny ... I've been shuffling pieces of paper on my table all morning. A certain order. Miky's white-tipped paws on the Bean's catalogue. Earlier I looked out the window and saw a big animal in the distance, white and dark brownish-olive. It was Miky staring at me from the steps ... my disordered imagination can make any scenario seem plausible ... The flame tree is pinky-orange, seems to be a shadow lying on the pink wall but is itself in shadow & I only know it's changed color because I saw it earlier. The kitchen window at a right angle from me is a perfect mirror for the dark grey maple tree shadow on the pink wall. I don't understand the optic rules for this.

NOVEMBER 18. A dimming, shrinking, of color (the flame tree). A concentration of brightness at the center of drying clusters of leaves, and the morning shadow falling over it, cast now by Gloria's house. Sun & shadow still on the brick wall. Sky slowly becoming overcast. A long vapor trail ... Interlude to look for pileated woodpecker dimensions in Petersen's. I'd disputed Sylvie's estimate of the one she'd seen. (held up her hands to about macaw-size). I was wrong—it is 16–18", the ivory bill 19–20".

NOVEMBER 19. The yellow rose still there seeming to become a little smaller & pointier. Flame tree bright against shady brick (overcast & wet snow predicted after rain) ... I woke up about 4:30 this morning, thought it was 6, had to pee repeatedly & wriggled & struggled with pillows & metallic end of bed ... Dream: *I hear birdsong loudly & clearly. I see a tree with bare branches covered with singing birds. I think I hear an oriole—& something with a trill like a goldfinch. Pure joy. I go to see Miss Balfour. She opens the door of her house & greets me, wearing white pajamas like my piqué ones, but only the shirt which comes down to her knees. She looks like herself, rather pale & welcoming. She must be about 65 & come to think of it, doesn't look quite like herself but I recognize her. Her face is wrinkled ...*

Dream: *Trudeau is with me, taking me for a drive, drives very fast over a curving up and downhill road. I say I'm scared when he goes so fast. He goes faster. In the rest of the dream other people are there but T. and I keep catching each other's eye in a mildly flirtatious way.*

SATURDAY, NOVEMBER 24. The peaceful death of the rose, one small petal held over its eye, and then violence: I fall down, cling to its slender vase, tip it over & there is water on the kitchen table, on the floor, the rose's petals are scattered. I am sitting in the corner, wedged between the yellow stool & the hard brick wall. I'd fallen on my seat and hit the back of my head hard against the wall. A big bump formed. First I managed to stretch my right leg out and hook my foot around the leg of the walker which for once hadn't fallen over. Then I got the reacher & reached the telephone and called Ann. She was there. I said it would take two people to get me up. She called Yvonne.[48] They both came, tugged hard under my arms & up I came like an elephant stuck in the mud. Both kind & gentle. Ann said, "Why didn't you press your Lifeline button? They would have called me." But they wouldn't have been able to get in. She said she might easily have been away. Her remedy which I don't like at all is to get Sylvie, Suzanne & Verena to come earlier. This squeezes very precious time alone down to about 1 hour working time. Rebellion brewing ... Flame tree fading with just a small topmost burst of pink-red—shrinking. But the temperature is still above zero at night (with exceptions). The 3 mauves on the kitchen table are perfect, more like tiny

48. Yvonne Klein, translator, editor, longtime friend and neighbor.

purple petunias with a waxy sheen, petals tidily spread out with faint radiating stripes. (true?) ...

Fallada is there, looking gravely down her nose. Verena says I must go out every day and breathe deeply. Last night the telephone rang in my dream and kept on ringing. I knew it was to tell me that Arthur had died. I wanted to say goodbye to him but woke up. It was a loud ring like the sound of birdsong the other night. Where do these sounds come from? Eliz. says there is nothing. A tangle of shadows on the wall. Have the tree men come? Branches still touching high-tension wires? Spruces, quince, rhododendron, clematis, still green.

NOVEMBER 25, SUNDAY. 12° C. this morning. L. woke me up at 6:30 & I still feel stupefied. Eyes prickle. Balance bad. And I got cross yesterday about everybody coming one hour longer. A power struggle with Ann but I hurt Sylvie's feelings. Impossible to let fly at one person and not hurt the nearest person's feelings ... Squirrel shadows chasing each other across the wall. Flame tree has lost all its leaves. Its leaves in the kitchen are dry & crumpled. Suzanne & I were going to write words on them—sluggish, uninspired. The irresistible tiredness. The great questions of the day: shall I wear my Polartec jacket during hair-washing? Kitchen is cold. I feel guilty about not going to see Joanna's show. Last day—warm & sunny. But Eleanor is coming with Sherry. I used to match wits with E., now can't even remember whom she interviewed last. Renata Adler. (Not to rub eyes.) To make whitecaps in the smooth passage of time. A feeling of self-hate. An authentic reason for guilt, I think. Today I think, where is Sylvie?

NOVEMBER 26. The limp feeling, eyes almost dropping shut, eyes prickling still. M.C. just called, back from Belgium. Dismal day. Flame tree leafless, pink rose very high & straight and green still ... Dream. *Verena has just been through a dreary winter & tells me that she's going to Italy in the spring & specially to Rome. I'm possessed by unbearable envy & the desire to say "Take me with you." Never gets said.*

NOVEMBER 27. Early morning, Miky has been moving very cautiously around & the room is light. I don't wake up till 6:55. *In my dream it's our birthday and I want to give Sarah some flowers—a bunch of orchids that I have to drive somewhere through the countryside to find ... I get the flowers; there is just one orchid. The rest are green leaves like my peace lily leaves. Sarah & I are together and we are driving home. We slip further and further to the right where the hill is steeper. I just manage to guide the car back up again, sideways, where it can't tip over* ... Not the first of its kind essentially about the feeling of losing my balance—the moment when it's too late to recover my balance. This happened this morning when E. was turning the white chair 45 degrees toward the sink but she had her arm firmly around me and gave up & I sat down heavily. -2° C. but green things are still green. Flame tree is leafless & invisible. It has tiny (scarlet) red berries that S. picks for table, for some reason they look like flowers.

NOVEMBER 28. Overcast. -2° again, snow predicted, specially tonight. Post-therapy day & I feel unsteady. Hand curled up, knee locks at every step. Last night I woke up at 2, wanted to pee, went to the bathroom, took 2 Tylenol & a very small fragment of Serax. Left leg had been twitching & I was afraid to lie on either side. Feet unbearably hot. Fell asleep about 5. Eliz. ever patient about bedpan. Hard to get to bathroom, knee locked, hand wouldn't uncurl. Yesterday M.C. and later, Cynthia for supper, delicious, that Suzanne left all prepared for us. M.C. had been to Brussels & Amsterdam, had seen Rita who talked about terrorist threat in the Netherlands. I felt the shakes coming over me again. M.C. says that the terrorists plan to destroy the whole non-Muslim world, have a fertile base in Amsterdam. Cynthia—brought one of her puddings. Told me about Carol Shields. The cancer is spreading. She is in Paris (?) where a farcical play of hers is being put on. Her husband is a geologist, has gone to London to study potholes. Could I have heard right? Muddled brain ... Suzanne just came in and has been talking to me about Leni Riefenstahl. The filmmaker for the glory of the Nazis and her ostracism & failure to find work after the war. The injustice of it. I try hard to think. What *do* I think? Sludge in my brain. Injustices, so many of them. Because she was a woman?

NOVEMBER 30. Could I feel limper than I do today? Getting up, no feeling in left foot except heat & difficulty walking—dragging, knee-locking, left hand crumpled up. Post-therapy! ... Dismal day, snow still on ground, clematis still green. But Marian coming. M.C. & Mouser have left for Key West ... Pink rose plant high & straight & summery green above fence ... M.C. yesterday—her straight little body, cheerful kindness & seriousness & self-confidence ... Her prime. Our funny little kisses, quick pecks, the same with Lise. Lise was reading *Lily Briscoe*. She said I was more feminist than B.D.[49] I said "Impossible!" She laughed at the octopus image—"that much-

49. Barbara Deming.

maligned egghead of the deep"—clasping people in her arms and sucking them dry. It just occurred to me that this may have hurt Bobbie's feelings ... Oh memories, the pressures of whom on whom, the perceptions of each, & no one to ask. My feeling now that my friendship with M.C. is sacred, can't be ruffled. She seems specially protected, reappears as she did on the beach, has the power of reappearance like Henrietta the cat. Though M.C. has never actually disappeared except in my disordered scenarios & incorrect remembering of what I've been told ...

Most dear Monser—
I don't think this is a very good self-portrait; I'm much more handsome and noble than this, mummy assures me. Between you and me she's too old to get a good likeness; it's behind her dimming powers. You and I know that cats are superior in every way to other beings including dogs though Mummy has a secret passim for dogs (slavishly attached to n'importe quel être humain—) And now that we're on the subject of secret passims how about Mummy and Lily. Sometimes I catch her looking yearningly out the window at Lily's tombstone and know that she's forgotten to think exclusively of me. But I'm making new friends: the little à tinge dyky CLSC nurse who coos to me and forgets to bug Mummy about getting a new mathess. I say to m— please keep the old one, it's right for me & that's what counts.

Marisa has Mummy going to Linda—something who can fix up the effects of strokes, etc.? heard M. explaining to Suzanne that she probably needs the prayers of all the dead conventional doctors in the family for faith in this far-out program— Maybe you could ask the advice of chanel & Sushi and Picasso. It's called iono-??? Much LOVE to you and Mum. I'll send you more boxes & self portraits—
XXX

❧

Most dear Mouser—

I don't think this is a very good self-portrait; I'm much more handsome and noble than this, Mummy assures me. Between you and me she's too old to get a good likeness; it's beyond her dimming powers. You and I know that cats are superior in every way to other beings including dogs though Mummy has a secret passion for dogs (slavishly attached to n'importe quel être humain). And now that we're on the subject of secret passions how about Mummy and Lily. Sometimes I catch her looking yearningly out the window at Lily's tombstone and know that she's forgotten to think exclusively of me. But I'm making new friends: the little a tinge dyky CLSC nurse who coos to me and forgets to bug Mummy about getting a new mattress. I say to M. please keep the old one, it's right for me and that's what counts.

Marisa has Mummy going to Linda something who can fix up the effects of strokes etc. I heard M. explaining to Suzanne that she probably needs the prayers of all the dead conventional doctors in the family for faith in this far-out program. Maybe you could ask the advice of Chanel & Sushi and Picasso. It's called iono-???

Much LOVE to you and Mum. I'll send you more faxes & self-portraits—

XXX

❧

DECEMBER 1. Snow gone. Everything green again, no flame tree leaves or autumn color left in the garden & a grey day about 3° C. Dream. *I'm on a stony beach—all white stones. I see some midway between spherical sand-dollars and sea urchins—beautiful—& pick 2 up to take home. The designs on them are clearly incised but I see that they're fossils. On the way home I fall down in the middle of the road and lie curled up ...*

DECEMBER 2, SUNDAY. Dream. *A big hotel. Each room has a German shepherd to guard it. I go to my room. The corridor is dark, I can't find my room—or the key? My dog isn't there ...*

DECEMBER 3. The arrival of packages. Beans, my lovely grey lightweight Polartec shirt and blue (light but not baby-blue) scarf and little glaring blue flashlight which I dislike and want to give away. Ellen Lee's wreath, doesn't have the deep balsamy smell that perfumes the house. *Why not?* Was it sprayed with green? Dark suspicions. But looks charming on rocking-horse, decked with red velvet ribbon.

DECEMBER 4. Sunny, blue sky with big clouds. Claire is here, padding softly around. I have the drugged feeling, just wrote "rhythm" instead of ribbon, "hear" for here. Last night I dreamt about Trudeau again. *I'd looked out of my groundfloor hotel window and seen a beautiful tiger standing in the empty street. No traffic. I signalled to someone, "Tiger. Come." Trudeau was with me, unfazed. His face was very rugged, bumpy all over.* I've forgotten what he said—just the impression of kind attention.

DECEMBER 8, SATURDAY. Gentle sunshine & blue sky the color of my new scarf. A constant coming & going of people today: Verena, Sylvie, Mary & Jim, Nina. Sleepiness. Agitation of the shadows on the wall—a squirrel has run along a thin branch. A new health nightmare—pressure sores—Mary wants to fit me with the latest gadget, this time a rigid foam collar about 3 inches wide. Eliz. tried it last night and after 1 minute I said take it off it cuts off my circulation. It bit into upper calf, right ... She wrapped a nice strip of padding around my leg & fastened it with a safety pin. Wakeful night while I imagined pressure sores in every likely part of my body & felt stabs of pain—imaginary? My heels, other ankle, seat. Miky heavily but thoughtfully fitted himself next to me. And then a wave of guilt about Sarah, of course; I can never let it go. A little comforted by memory of "my Mary." I clutch at that.

DECEMBER 14. 2°. Overcast with sun quietly gaining strength. Dream. *I look out the door of a square clapboard frame house. It's raining steadily and flood-waters have risen all the way to the doorsill. I realize that all the pictures downstairs will be deep in water. Sarah is floundering in the cellar and I jump in and begin to drown.* And wake up. This part was almost erased when I woke up and I have a feeling of having invented it. Earlier in the night I asked E. for the bedpan & then had the impression that it was much too far forward. "It's all wet," said E. about the bed. Pajama pants damp but not soaking ... Today on the verge of dizziness. O energy ...

❧

Dear and admired Mouser,

I found this picture of Lily exercising her charms. She and you were friends, I remember, and she treated you with suitable respect. How Mummy misses the subtlety of her character without appreciating the robust boyishness of mine. I like to put my wet nose close to her ear and chew on her hair and she doesn't appreciate how lucky she is to get this token of my affection. Oh Mouser, I can say this only to you, she will always prefer Lily to me.

Well, this is supposed to be Mummy's day of revelation. She'll be able to hear what I'm saying to her, my priceless words. I open my mouth often but the poor old thing doesn't hear a thing, though others tell me that I sound like all four tenors together when I want my special dinner.

Fallada looks very nice with snow all down her nose. She's the iron horse on the blue gate. How she hated being in all winter.

Happy Christmas dear Mouser. Maybe Mum will give you a piece of turkey …

Much much love

DECEMBER 26.[50] Journal nowhere to be seen. Dream: *I've painted a whole lot of almost abstract pictures, unlike anything I've ever done and preliminary drawings in color of lines scrawled loosely across the white paper—I'm showing them to Jane Gapen who doesn't like them. I burst out, "There isn't a single one you've liked!" I can't see her but she's there.* This is about my complete absence of belief in myself these days, hard not to run myself down all the time ... Drowned in Christmas mail. I haven't written in my journal, can't even find it. Tidying stirs everything up and more things get lost. Loretta & I out-tidy ourselves. Yesterday—full of activities—tidying, going upstairs to look for painting with sheep in it, hair-washing. Exhaustion. Memory very bad. When I called Sylvie A. she said I'd already called her. This gave me pause, to say the least; how many times have I done this? Hearing-aid kept going off & I couldn't hear telephone had to switch to left hand, very awkward. K.H. called & I kept rambling on; she was clearly relieved when I said goodbye ... The lame & awkward (& hoarse) conversation with Paishy, Aaron, Dixie, Heidi, Robbie (couldn't hear Heidi & Robbie seemed to get crosser & crosser) ... Despair when I hung up. Galloping senility? Today my memory has come back but I'm awfully sleepy. I sit here with my eyes closed drooling (inadvertently). A light-blue sky & mild sunshine. Two squirrel shadows chasing each other on the brick wall and reflected in the kitchen window. Upside down. Very nice. Diary peeping out—only empty since Dec. 14. 12 days.

DECEMBER 27. Dream: *I'm standing next to a woman in a white cotton dress, belted—like the uniforms in* The Handmaid's Tale—*and a little white cap like maids' caps in the 17th & 18th centuries. She steps out the window and falls 12 stories to the ground. Without thinking I step out, too, and fall, hit the ground & wake up, surprised to be still alive and unhurt.* What's it all about? I'm moving at a snail's pace today.

⤳

Me voilà, cher Mouser, beau comme tabby champion que je suis, pas racé comme toi bien sur mais avec la distinction de je ne sais qui qui vient du feu Baker Road. Moi-même, Miky, suis un peu *couch potato*— je n'aime pas les petites boules de neige entres mes orteils comme du sorbet à la vanille. *Hagendaaz. I must say you live a charmed life down there. Imagine the bad manners of Gloria's black cat who comes over here and pees under the porch to avoid the snow, I suppose. And in the summer*

50. On looseleaf yellow paper.

she digs holes among the tender plants Verena has put in, to ... I can't say the word. Even old Mummy stuck bricks, slates & hunks of wood in every bare space to discourage her & her disorderly friends over there.

Mummy says her mind is crowded with detritus like an old rusty spigot and she doesn't have any memorable dreams anymore. She and I sleep silently side by side.

As I said, Mum has lost her touch. Delectable smells are wafting from the kitchen where Suzanne is creating masterpieces. Much love and kisses to everybody from Mike & his ancient Mummy.

❧

Me voilà, que je suis chez Monson, beau comme tabby champion suis, pas racé comme toi, bien mais avec la distinction de je ne sais qui gui vient du feu Baker Road, Moi-même, Miky, suis un peu couch potato; je n'ai pas les petites boules de neige entre mes orteils comme du 30z bot de la vanille Hazandass. I must say you live a charmed life down there. Imagine the bad manners of cat who here and pees porch to avoid the snow. Gloria's black comes over under the I suppose — And in the summer she digs holes among the tender plants Verena has put in, to .... I can't say the word — Even old mummy stuck bricks, slates & hunks of wood in every bare space to discourage her & her disorderly friends over there — Mummy says her mind is crowded with detritus like an old rusty spigot and she doesn't have any memorable dreams anymore. She and I sleep silently side by side — As I said, Mummy has lost her touch — Dilectable smells are wafting from the Kitchen where Suzanne is creating — masterpieces. and Kisses to Much love everybody from Mike & his ancient mummy

SUNDAY, DECEMBER 30. Snow! Big abundant flakes. Last night couldn't get Elizabeth Bishop tape to work & read little book. So far difficult poems ("The Man-moth," for instance) I've never been able to understand. Worse than ever now. Slow in the head. A sense of inadequacy. I can still observe & remember details—the texture & increased pinkness of the failing roses P. & S. gave me, the tenacious & pinky white one from Judy seeming to close again with the others (perhaps it should be alone?). In E.B. everything means something else. I try to remember how she was with M.C. and me. Always uncomplicated. The drama of the crack in the blue finger bowl still roils in my head. I still argue and protest. "But I didn't know there was a crack"—the terrible image & I was bound to it. But E. invited me to come to Maine, to Ouro Preto—yes, I must think of this. And with this peaceful thought the snow stopped when I wasn't looking. An aching longing to have been spoken of somewhere by her, without bad feeling ...

JANUARY 2, 2002. (Jan. 1. uneventful ... Yvonne stopped in, Joanna, Suzanne washed my hair. Total collapse ... Did lackluster therapy exercises ...)

Another powder blue cloudless day. -10°, says thermometer, radio said -5°. Or maybe that's high. My sloppiness of listening. Listened attentively (I thought) to Elizabeth Bishop. Her voice nice and loud but as she says in little book flat and unbeautiful. And I have to read poems, see words, reread— and still don't always understand. It was always like this, a sudden running into fog. "The Man-moth." Does it help to know it comes from the misprinted "mammoth"? Yesterday a sudden wish to write about old age.

The present interrupts. I see a bird sitting on the snow. A sudden jerk and it is pulled upward by its stem ... Death—represented in the *BMC Alumnae Register 2001* by two tiny dots ... (sometimes only one: why?) ... For something so momentous. A sign to represent an absence ... two tiny dots. For some reason I thought about Winnie, her small, pale, beautifully fine and delicate hands. Her gloves, her wrist warmers and nubbly handknitted caps like woolen shower caps. Important to have an image that can come back in dreams.

Balsam smell. Stephen said balsam firs are being bred with Frasier firs that have much less smell but last longer, don't drop their needles, etc. This year's is still green, has no smell and hasn't dropped its needles. Sacrilege!

JANUARY 3. All I remember of a dream last night is digging out of the sand— *first a smooth black (like lignum vitae) bowl about 5" diameter. I clean the sand (fine white sand, dampish) off it, then dig out a polished ball about as big as a croquet ball and carefully clean it off & put it in the bowl, very pleased with myself,* & wake up.

For a long time, I see, i.e. since before November, I've had the limp easy-fall-down feeling almost as soon as I get up. An obligatory lack of focus. Much concentration on writing words without making mistakes. Not old age at work but something like the wax in my ears, blurring, distorting. Was Vivaldi's *Stabat Mater* really so worn that it was defective or was my right ear hearing the recording that way? And yet Mozart's *467* was wonderfully clear … Imaginary illnesses—the ones that make sense, qualify—memory loss. Amy Tan and her mother—the weight of her mother's voice, wrenched from the shadows of her mind to testify to the truth, the urgent need to remember *those* words, when a feature of memory loss is that words *do not come* when they are called but have to wait for some working of signals. Forgetfulness is not selective. Why *Pandora?* Why remember it? It is there like a note in perfect pitch. Pandora, Patricia. Now it's like a train going from light into a dark tunnel. I'm trying to think of the name of Sylvie's partner (Dutch) and the train bursts out with a coming of light & a lessening of the clattering sound over rails—as the word Pandora comes into light: RITA.

JANUARY 5, SATURDAY. Days sliding by. I have the slowly tipping over feeling—to the left. I can still put on a sort of brake, some muscle over my left buttock & hip, but it starts again in its slyly suggestive way. A pressure between left elbow and chair arm & squeezing down of elbow …

JANUARY 7. *A dream about stacking dusty, crumbling old paintings tidily in the corner of an attic.* Yesterday Peter Poor called to tell me about Annie's[51] fall. Pure panic before. In the hospital, pelvic fracture & rehabilitation to come. His voice a little creaky like an old man & I realized how long it's been since I've last seen him—40 years?

JANUARY 9. Today—self-centered, whiny, with no humor; I dislike myself intensely. A bad D. accident. The sequence of getting my underpants, Polartec pants, shoes off—wash, wash pants by dangling them in toilet with reacher, not smear shit on everything, get dressed again (put leg in the wrong pant leg 3 times) … Collapse & exhaustion all day, minimal exercises. Tried M.'s wrist brace, heavy & hard to put on. Designed for weightlifting, too? Must be 2–3 lbs.

51. Annie Poor, painter, old friend.

This morning as hard to get up as ever. Arm doesn't want to unbend, hand has to be pulled open. Foot unpredictable. Constant vigilance, *not to fall*. The day—everything motionless except the quick flick of a squirrel's tail. Yesterday a sparrow flew up and away, I swear that this really happened ... Today, possible freezing rain & the terror of ice. Sleepy feeling beginning. Such stillness outside that even a snowflake would remain suspended in the air. The turgid flow of blood in my veins. But old age is at work the way hair and fingernails & toenails grow after death. The flesh becoming compost. I think of Lily curled up so comfortably, being reduced to her feathery fur. Her tombstone hidden under the snow.

FROM: MIKE, oh dear,   TO: MOUSER

Mouser, I'm so sleepy - It's another of those days pale and glum and even Gloria's open door & cat chow doesn't tempt me - Mammy feels sleepy, too, poor old thing. I wish I'd seen those 2 Prg Dogs you saw on Jan. 6. Were they like the wriggly little what's his name who was the apple of Paul Chavchavadge's eye? Nushka? Yesterday Enaki came and I made myself scarce though he's been very polite and aloof lately - He lies out on the porch and rolls his eyes meaningfully ... I read this morning in the Lynx (the Zorlogical Society Bulletin) that a member had seen a seagull drop out of the sky (dead, I'm sorry to tell you) from eating pure chocolate - I told that to Mummy and she said, "I knew it!" There were about 50 other dead seagulls - It seems chickadees like plain doughnuts, better than suet - I like a little goat's milk cheese every now and then. Sylvie just came with some delicious soup for Mummy - I must say that woman (Mummy) is outrageously spoiled - Why doesn't anybody bring me soup? I'm getting sick of my special diet! And I'm probably older than old Mummy and deserve some gourmet cooking -.. I'll write you again when I feel less like a pillowcase full of lead weights, xxx to you & & your dear Mum. Mr. Beam sounds nice -

Thanks for the beautiful foto David Steward called Mummy yesterday & I think he on B his parts on the head would project the moon & planets.

Oh dear, Mouser, I'm so sleepy. It's another of those days pale and glum and even Gloria's open door & cat chow doesn't tempt me. Mummy feels sleepy, too, poor old thing. I wish I'd seen those 2 pug dogs you saw on Jan. 6. Were they like the wriggly little what's his name who was the apple of Paul Chavchavadge's eye? Yesterday Enuki came and I made myself scarce though he's been very polite and aloof lately. He lies out on the porch and rolls his eyes meaningfully ... I read this morning in the Lynx (the Zoological Society Bulletin) that a member had seen a seagull drop out of the sky (dead, I'm sorry to tell you), from eating pure chocolate. I told that to Mummy and she said, "I knew it!" There were about 50 other dead seagulls. It seems chickadees like plain doughnuts better than suet. I like a little goat's milk cheese every now and then.

Sylvie just came with some delicious soup for Mummy. I must say that woman (Mummy) is outrageously spoiled. Why doesn't anybody bring me soup? I'm getting sick of my special diet. And I'm probably older than old Mummy and deserve some gourmet cooking ... I'll write you again when I feel less like a pillowcase full of lead weights.

X X X to you & your dear Mum

JANUARY 10. ... Wister's 87th birthday. He seems very much alive today, I hear his voice. The recollection of sound, the uncanny hearing of a movement of a Mozart or Beethoven concerto just before playing the CD. Beethoven, *No. 2*, last night, not exact or complete like the Mozart but accurate enough to recognize ... Judy ... the inseparable elephants she'd seen on TV. They had met again after 30 years of separation and couldn't contain their joy, went around with closely twined trunks. An English woman who first took a baby orphaned elephant into her house (made a special door for it) and then the friend her elephant had been separated from ...

LEFT HAND

JANUARY 14. Annie died the night of Jan. 12th ... Peter called me yesterday morning. She died very quietly, he said, had stopped eating, as if she decided to die. She was ready perhaps, couldn't fight anymore to live, our indomitable Annie who had survived so many near-deaths. And I think of other deaths like hers, from pneumonia. First a fall, then pneumonia ... Incurable. But was nobody there? Not Peter, no. Anna? Another huge absence. But for once no reproaches, no piercing guilt.

JANUARY 15. When Peter called he said that *Annie asked him to call me*. A farewell? Of course I'm already writing a scenario. But I know we were important to each other. I remember our walk in the woods at New City when I longed to say "I love you," and was silent, afraid she'd be displeased. The fear of being thought ridiculous, a poison. But blurting out love can mean banishment—light mockery.

This morning the sun made an isolated patch of bright yellow-orange on the trunk of the Dolgo apple that looked like a fresh blaze with an axe—quite deep. I thought, this means that the tree will be cut down in the spring because it interferes with the power lines. Typical of my implausible scenarios. And I saw Sandy's star as a big crow.

JANUARY 17. Snow all morning ending in flakes almost too fine to see ... And a hint of sun. Fallada's face is entirely white.

JANUARY 20, SUNDAY. Markale's *L'Épopée Celtique d'Irlande* all morning. Marvellous. I see I've made mistakes in illustrations. Does it matter? Thrilling stories of horses & their loyalty ...

JANUARY 23. *Unbecoming*. I thought of this word as a description of old age, a gradual disintegration and loss of self except for the core, a selfish self who has a hard time thinking of others with the same intensity, *sticking* to the image of another person. Particularly Annie. I think of her loud, clear, decided voice of this last year, as though she had concentrated all her energies under a powerful microscope. So different from my own hoarse, faltering voice which refuses to say the words I want it to say, blocked, it seems, by phlegm and saliva. The saliva actually drips from my mouth or nose in a clear drop (this happened with Susanne H.), so I carry a piece of Kleenex to dab at it. And remember drops falling down Arthur's nose without his seeming to notice. Compulsory slow motion. With every step a scenario for falling unreels. I'll be ready, I think. Which one cannot be? The most that one can hope for is to have an empty chair-seat handy. There is a second of unconsciousness when 1) one sneezes, 2) the doorbell rings, the telephone rings.

JANUARY 28. Another mild day & pale sun. SW wind, they say. Commanding sleepiness goes on and on; a sort of binding non-energy. Doesn't come with pills, it precedes them. Prevents me from thinking. I seem to be under a spell, just able to function. In a dream last night I had to stand in front of a big audience and make a cheerful speech. I felt cheerful and full of pep. Woke up just as I began to talk. I was younger & rather plump ... I feel the absence of anyone I could talk to who knew Annie. There are so many questions about her sickness & death I want to ask. And I don't even have Peter's telephone number. And not a very accurate memory of her physical presence. Accurate memories, living and dead: Ruth, warm, Sarah, rather formal. M.C., a family-type hug and quick hard kiss on the mouth, Claire & Sylvie, warm & nice, Suzanne, courtly, graceful.

JANUARY 29, TUESDAY. New mattress just arrived. Mattress has 4 cylinders of air somewhere inside that have to be pumped up now & then. One can't sit on it for a long time, my head always has to be west end ... Lucile & Suzanne upstairs now photographing *Wide Sargasso Sea*. Cynthia gave me a tiny slug of the Balvenie—instant wobbly feeling but I slept almost without moving till 5 AM on the new very firm mattress & my feet didn't hurt. This morning as sleepy as ever & my eyes prickle. Vision far-sighted. Cynthia found CBC after much struggle; kept saying "Shoot!" wanted me to listen to Peter Gzowski. She looked beautiful. V. enthusiastic about *Cuchulainn* & *Jane Eyre*.[52] Liked C.'s two horses and the intensity of C.'s violence (my depiction of) ... thoughts don't materialize. And now winter is coming with thermometer plunging and lots of snow (just as M.C. gets here). This morning early, the insistent images of elephants being dropped out of cargo planes in Vietnam by U.S. forces, their legs splintering like matchwood ("their bones have the tensile strength of celery"—Shana Alexander) and their all dying in horrible agony. This was the U.S. solution to the problem of transport along the Ho Chi Minh Trail.

JANUARY 30. All my feeling now seems to be going into stricken grief for animals and for Annie, my inability to reach her. As though she were being

52. Mary created watercolor illustrations in the late '60s and early '70s for stories of the Irish hero Cuchulainn as well as for *Jane Eyre* and *Wide Sargasso Sea*.

deliberately kept distant from me. Peter—so nice, but what is he telling me what is he withholding? And the calm news from Vera that both Gardner and Ruth have died. My non-connection with the next generation, except for my own. Logan, great-grandniece, present through photographs.

FEBRUARY 5. Already—my usual cranky feeling when I wake up from a nap, dissatisfaction with myself, recollection of failures of attention to nice people. Claudia today. Unbecoming. This word that slides out of my head, or that ...

FEBRUARY 6. Eyes hurt today ... big lazy snowflakes. I see the pale edges of a squirrel's curved tail on the Dolgo apple in front of the brick wall ... *Chicken Run* drove me crazy. All movement & frenetic talk that I couldn't quite hear, the elastic beaks not like chickens. So I had to turn it off. I decided that I'm much too slow for the new age and should stick to my leisurely program of almost no TV, books like *The Astonishing Elephant* & natural history, and calm, nonchoral music. Suzanne brought her French translation of *Alice in Wonderland* today with illustrations by a Czech painter, very elaborate and colorful. My criterion is always Tenniels's, which seem to have grown out of the story; the characters can *only* look like that is my view—and almost anybody would say that this is narrow-minded, that old people can't accept change. And now I know this is true, that we are emotionally bonded to our childhood books and images, that that is our truth. Tenniels's cheshire cat *is* the cheshire cat, a real cat with a real cat's smile ... But can't there be another truth that would be suitable for our time? ... I think it's easier for us to imagine ourselves into Victorian or Shakespearean time if it's consistent than to wrench the original to make it fit contemporary (our) time.

FEBRUARY 8. Bright sun. Pieces of my body aren't articulated, as if there were gaps of consciousness. Nothing new but more pronounced today, it seems. And my eyes hurt ...

FEBRUARY 11. A cold day (to be -9° all day) with bright sun & piercing wind. Miky didn't show up & I began to get worried. "Oh, he's eating," said Leonie casually. Last night she ... shoved Miky off my bed brusquely when she brought the bedpan. The poor old soul had been snuggled close to me & I concocted all sorts of scenarios when he didn't come in the bathroom this morning. He'd gone upstairs. Usually he comes to watch very gravely while my feet are washed, shoes put on, etc. Now he's curled up on the kitchen table. A terrible sinking feeling when I make my death-scenarios ...

Feb. 11

Dear Mouser—how are you? How is your poor ailing Mum? At least she is away from this sad white landscape with black dead-looking bushes that make my Mum groan and lament. I don't feel like going out even to look for something to eat at Gloria's whose house is cold and dark. So I curl up on Mum's new mattress most of the day. Suzanne puts me around her neck and kisses me every day and Mum is unusually nice to me and doesn't tell me all the time how much she misses Lily.

Please feel better soon, say Mum and I in unison and harmony. Verena has it, too, and sounds awful on the telephone and is too sick with it to give her therapy.

Mopingly with much love,

your friend Mike and Mum

Feb 11, '02

Dear Mouser — how are you? How is your poor ailing Mum? At least she is away from this sad white landscape with black dead-looking bushes that make my Mum groan and lament I don't feel like going out even to look for something to eat at Gloria's whose house is — cold and dark. So I curl up on Mum's new mattress most of the day. Suzanne puts me around her neck and kisses me every day and Mum is unusually nice to me and doesn't tell me all the time how much she misses Lily —

Please feel better soon, say Mum and I in unison and harmony. Verena has it, too, and sounds awful on the telephone and is too sick with It to give her therapy —

Cynthia is coming to supper —

Mopingly with much love, your friend Mike and Mum

FEBRUARY 15. Dream: *I'm sitting at the top of a curving beach. A whole group of sunburned young men—some kind of club—come noisily over the curve. A big elephant is padding along freely in front of them; he seems to be coming angrily toward me. I stand up, bow respectfully and say, "O mighty elephant!" He or she stops, looks at me with a funny little curling of the lip (that expression that elephants and various other animals have in common—mountain sheep? I've seen it in a documentary).* The first dream I've had about an animal for a long time.

The kind of day that seems as though a light is turned up on the inside— a pale sunshine. My imminent feeling of capsizing. Yesterday Lise came for freewriting. Gertrude Stein—writing freely herself, it seems. Strange how my turgid brain always seems to produce something that is faintly witty. "Frustrated dormant worker bees in my head waiting for some reason to unlock the signal for life."

FEBRUARY 16, SATURDAY. Betsy,[53] Susan and Leif just stopped in to leave their bags, went for breakfast at the Gascogne & are coming back soon. Leif walks beautifully and is a real little boy. Betsy looks wonderful, like her old self. Two miracles of determination and defiant hope that awes me. Betsy with her old ringing voice, her *joie de vivre* ...

FEBRUARY 17. Light fine snow & sun struggling to get through—a sort of trembling of snow in the air.

∼

Feb. 22

Oh ye gods, Mouser, peerless catpal, why does Mum waste her time doing these inferior portraits of me? She should retire gracefully like other self-respecting persons of nearly 85.

I have perfectly adequate & well-sharpened claws but Joanna puts me on her lap (on my back) and utters endearments in my ear and I'm as it were hypnotized and gaze at her like Samson with his hair. Delilah probably had very nice hair herself that I would have liked to nest in but better to bring down a temple. Cats have always influenced history as the footnotes have told us. Search your soul, Mouser, does your Mummy give cats enough room in her majesterial opus? With this thought I will say ciaou since Mum & Loretta are practicing their somewhat halting italiano. Much faithful & eternal love to you and your dear Mummy.

∼

53. Betsy Warland.

O ye gods, mouser, peerless cat pal, why does Mum waste her time doing these in- ferior por- traits of me? She should retire gracefully like

Feb 22 '02

other self-respecting persons of nearly 85 — I have perfectly adequate & well-sharpened claws but Joanna puts me on her lap (on my back) and utters endearments in my ear and I'm as it were hypnotized and gaze at her like Samson with his hair - Delilah probably had very nice hair herself, that I would have liked to nest in but better to bring down a temple - Cats have always influenced history as the footnotes have told us! Search your soul, Mouser, does your Mummy give cats enough room in her majesterial opus? With this thought I will say ciaou since Mum & Loretta are practising their somewhat halting italiano. Much faithful eternal love to you and your dear Mummy.

SUNDAY, FEBRUARY 24. Grudging, unsteady movement, vague eyesight, sleepiness. Fell asleep at table just now & M.C. called ... Sylvie & I going over notebooks from 1930's to '90's ... Notes from Dr. Chew's class in The Romantics to elaborate thoughts about books & plays ... Poems and dreams, very long and complicated sometimes & full of Freudian sexual images. I crossed out a lot of things with impenetrable India ink & tore out pages. A lot of self-censorship has been going on all my life, unregretted, except for all the paintings I destroyed. Now is the time for uncensored sounds, some permissible, some forbidden in polite society: belch, fart, heartburn, hiccup, cough, sneeze (loudly), drool (soundless but more & more uncontrollable, rolls down the corners of my mouth, falls off my collar). Yesterday after my nap I spent a long time trying to straighten up to a sitting position and kept toppling over. It reminded me unpleasantly of pre-stroke inability to sit up when I was lying on the grass after our canoe trip ...

FEBRUARY 25. A long dream last night began & continued in a huge earth-lined black cavern littered with little pieces of trash small enough to stick to one's clothes. *The first thing I do is to cut out a piece of my heart and wait for a surgeon to come along. He does not come. It is painless, my knife is very sharp like the knives in the hallucinations. A lot of men come along, shabby & threatening or quite friendly. There is only one woman. Gradually everything is taken away from me except the dark green wallet which I manage to keep hidden. But I have memories of being pawed over and scared. This dream goes on and on & resumes after I pee. The conspicuous thing is that the cavern seems to get dirtier all the time & my clothes get more torn & shabby. I end in a long black cloth raincoat almost to the floor, ragged at the bottom. The doctor never shows up.*

FEBRUARY 27. Dream image (last night): *As usual I'm in a closed-in space, this time a university perhaps, walking through it. I cross a center for handicapped children. One of them close to me has two faces, one above the other—a child's face and the face of a middle-aged person.* This gives me the horrors and I'm still haunted by it—though it seems like a harmless image of childhood becoming middle age.

MARCH 1. Another of those grey ambiguous days, sun hidden, 2° or is it still -2°. So lovely to see Martine's[54] beautiful kindly face yesterday. She's cut her hair, not drastically but it changes her appearance & makes it a little more austere ... Trouble with my hearing-aid again with the three of us. And Loretta discovered that it wasn't quite in the hearing canal. Martine talked about the ordeal of coming out to her family, relatively non-violent. Father the most opposed, Mother understanding, siblings too. Later I had thoughts about my conversation with Verena in which I tried to explain why I didn't want to celebrate my 85th birthday. Not a cause for celebration, I said, to be a pampered prisoner of a body that can do less and less. My chief joy is in eating and in seeing beloved friends who never bully me ... But it is *not* an accomplishment to reach the age of 85. My siblings were less lucky. I'm

54. Martine Giguère, carpenter and friend.

orphaned. It occurred to me that this period of being alive while my family and friends like Annie are dead is like a pre-purgatory during which I can review every sin of thoughtlessness, cruelty, violence, extreme impatience; absence of compassion, hate (on and on) along with excessive humility and cowardice. Leaving out always evidence of kindness, generosity, humor—all good qualities ("that you have when you're in a good mood or have had some success," says the little inner voice). Reading *Graham Greene on Capri* by Shirley Hazzard—my life there comes back with crystal clarity, specially the jaundice period, of course (the time when I was a dreary impediment. The cold tile floor under my feet, did I have a bedpan?). Thinking now of the contempt G.G. would have had for me, a lesbian with literary pretenses who was ignorant about the world and didn't love men and painted delicate little watercolors ... Did he have an affair with Letizia? He would have fascinated me with his indifference to landscape, flowers, painting, music, the opposite of D.H. Lawrence in many ways. Did they meet? I must ask Judy ...

MARCH 2, SATURDAY. Sleepiness down to my fingertips and in my back. My eyes close, I take a little cat nap and feel even sleepier.

MARCH 3. Another melancholy day and the feeling of moving through a medium as heavy as mercury. Could it be a urinary infection? ... A nice visit yesterday by Eleanor with work by Urqui (?) poets exiled in London where she's going soon to interview them ... This morning I read about Greene's feeling in his 80's that he'd outlived all his friends & Hazzard's quotation from Wordsworth about Coleridge's death. The only key to entry into a man's world for a woman is faithful passion without envy for a man ...

MARCH 4. Dream. *Father materializes in a dark coat like a raincoat and just stands silently without looking at me.* Later I read a review of a book about Spinoza and think of Father's interest in him and think how close now his philosophy is to my own. God as universe, not a Christian god. One with the whole of creation. How Spinoza was hated and accused by Christians. How much I wish now that I'd discussed his ideas with Father, who dutifully went to church with Mother. His silent presence in my dream.

March 4

Oh cruellest month, in the generosity of our Canadian hearts we have probably sent another cold wave down there & you and your mum are shivering. My mummy and I are in a state of GLOOM because yesterday it was +10° and this morning it was -15°. It's too cold even to go over to Gloria's and recharge my batteries with her junk food. It makes me feel sick but she says she just loves cats. Sometime in her next life she will pay for it ...

March 9, 2002

Dear Mouser,

Thank you or maybe it was your Mum who sent this Modigliani day up here in answer to our prayers and sun-dances. They say it will go up to 17° this but then afternoon will a big wind come and tomorrow will be cold again Oh, shiver my white whiskers, will spring come at last??? The little spruce tree is quite green I must say —

Mum thanks you profusely for that far package which will pad many lean months. She spends futile hours worrying about lean months when Ed assures her that there won't be any, the Dow Jones index is climbing again, etc. Marian called her just now and said Ed has started building his gazebo for Sarah which sounds just lovely. It has a 150 year old school bell in a sort of dome & looks out on a beautiful landscape. Love & XXX to you & your dear Mum from me Mike & old you-know-who XXX

SAL-UT Mouser et sa Mum

March 9

Dear Mouser,

Thank you or maybe it was your Mum who sent this prodigious day up here in answer to our prayers and sun-dances. They say it will go up to 17° this afternoon but then a big wind will come and tomorrow will be cold again. Oh, shiver my white whiskers, will spring come at last??? The little spruce tree is quite green I must say— ...

MARCH 10. SUNDAY. *March*—a cold word, sharp-edged, not like *May*. Suggests goosestep, a crisp rhythmical beat. This morning I noticed that in yesterday's *Gazette* "brooch'" was spelled "broach." Strange how offensive a misspelling can be. One's attention is violently jerked to the word *broach* and its double meaning, so far from *brooch*. Meaning: the identity not of sound but of something *seen*. Suddenly outside a snow shower a dense grey curtain —when I wasn't looking—replaced mild sunshine & pale blue sky. Tapering off. A light coat on railing, sundial, frog. None on Fallada. Windy, sun filtered through light cloud cover.

MARCH 11. A glorious day, cloudless, cold again, -10° at 7, climbing up ... Ann coming 2:30, Cynthia coming 5:30. Ann has found an ophthalmologist to replace Dr. C. I have a tendency to oppose automatically whatever A. proposes, then I come around. Like Mother. Dream. *I'm in a big gothic building with lots of people and Miky. I'm packing, leaving for somewhere. The question is whether to leave Miky behind. I feel anguish ...* Today oppressively sleepy as usual. Woke up trembling but got over it with a conscious effort ... Yesterday twice I got to the toilet too late to prevent a sort of preliminary peeing, not enough to change pants but enough to depress me and make me feel out of control.

Yesterday Sylvie lugged my wonderful wooden tool box upstairs and we looked at everything: beef bones, beans (nikker and sandalwood), beads, small rasps, the fine metal saw, the tool that puts out a fine claw that will pick up fragments of bone, etc., the tiny vise that screws shut, opens to 3/4", the Dremel attachments, things I couldn't identify anymore, thrilling to see. S. very excited & happy. As an artist her tastes & skills are closest to mine, though she's more inventive and patient. And meticulous. As she is with plants. An ability to talk to them like someone who is immediately acknowledged by animals.

11:15. Miky appeared from nowhere to greet Suzanne who held him close with his paws over her shoulders.

MARCH 12. The drama of the dead rat. Eliz. comes into the bathroom and says, "There's a dead rat in the living room." Her face is pale green. I say, "Rock?" "No, RAT." I don't understand. She says she'll tell me later. Later she says very plainly, "There's a dead RAT in the living room. Do you want to see it?" Me: "Yes, of course." Feeling slightly sick. She brings the rat in on a plant dish like the head of John the Baptist—a real rat—grey, about 7 inches long with no sign of wounds or blood on it. Evidently Mike brought it upstairs when I wasn't looking & laid it under the table. I remembered the sounds I heard downstairs of some creature yelling—a mouse I thought ... I suggested to Eliz. to put it in the outgoing garbage which she did. When Claire came I told her about the rat and she gasped with horror, on the verge of screaming. I said it was lucky she wasn't here & she said that she would have started smoking again, a terrible thought ...

⌒

Very respected Prince Mouser—your Mum just called & my Mum was making this awful picture of me, the aristocrat of la race parisienne. Do you remember that place where we got darling doomed Tidi? And the somewhat dubious woman who ran it? Now everybody is making a fuss about my rat whom I presented out of pure love to Mum. Too bad she didn't find him. Elizabeth turned a sort of green but she brought him to show Mum on a plate like the head of St. Jean Baptiste. Human beings are apt to be a little bit hysterical at the sight of a rat. I remember Mum saying that some innocent fruitrats used to gnaw holes in the screens at the cottage (Sugarloaf) and forage around for things to eat. They had beautiful reddish fur but Blue used to put out Have-a-Heart traps & take them far away. I have to say that Mum doesn't adore rats the way she pretends to, in fact she was scared that one would jump on her bed and take a bite out of her toe ... Much love—

⌒

/ Mar. 12, 2002 /

Very respected Prince Mouser — Your Mum this just called & my Mum was making an awful picture of me, the aristocrat of la race parisienne — Do you remember that place where we got darling doomed Tidi? And the somewhat dubious woman who ran it? Now everybody is making a fuss about my rat whom I presented out of pure love to Mum Too bad she didn't find him — Eliz-abeth turned a sort of green but she brought him to show Mum on a plate like the head of St. Jean Baptiste — Human beings are apt to be a little bit hysterical at the sight of a rat. I remember Mum saying that some innocent fruit rats used to gnaw holes in the screens at the cottage (Sugarloaf) and forage around for things to eat They had beautiful reddish fur but Blue used to put out Have-a-Heart traps & take them far away. I have to say that Mum doesn't adore rats she way she pretends to, in fact she was scared that one would jump on her bed and take a bite out of her toe — I'd like to go along on your walks with Mary-Claire & her Mum & Dad & you — Much love

MARCH 14. The dreaded ultrasound was barely dreadful at all, no x-ray, just a probe that roved over my abdomen with the aid of a smeary substance, the Dr. pressing rather hard and an image appearing on a screen. At the end he said it was very good; S. said this meant only that I'd been good about obeying his instructions to hold a deep breath & breathe normally ... Today I feel sleepy as usual, and depressed for no good reason. A bubbling delight only in dreams. Strange women kissing me warmly and unexpectedly ...

3/15

Oh goodness me, dear Mouser, is it true about the hen and her chicks in the street? You must remember that only circumstantial evidence links me to that rat, though I remember chasing it around the cellar and thinking, here's something that Mum would really like ... Your fax yesterday was beautiful. By the way, my rat was grey like an enormous mouse. Loretta & Mum agreed that they don't like mice setting up house in their bureau drawers. Poor Loretta had grippy symptoms yesterday but just called up to say she's coming. It's supposed to rain, sleet, freeze, blow—not fit for a comfort-loving cat like me. So I spend the day on Mum's bed. I do her the favor every now and then nibble her hair and pull it to see if she's still alive and she says, go away. Oh, the tragic rejection of my love.

I wish I could send you a joyous drawing of spring foliage but all I see is the little leafless pendulata whipping around in the wind.

Love and kisses—Mike and his Mum

08/15/02

SATURDAY, MARCH 16. Sunny blue sky. After reading about Kierney's death at breakfast I began to mourn for Lily again: her head tucked under my arm and Emily with her nose lying on my knee as we drove to the kennels before I went to France and heard when I got back that she'd been operated on for cancer and was put to sleep. The memories of touch of both Emily and Lily. E.'s silky black head and the almost raspy short hairs above Lily's nose & just under her eyes. Hair that never grew. The passion of love, pure love, it seems, one feels for an animal ...

SUNDAY, MARCH 17. St. Patrick's Day. Cold bright cloudless blue sky. Last night Sylvie's palpable disappointment when she called the MFA and was told that the tickets for the land art film were sold out. It was about a Scottish land artist. They work with stones, rivers & other natural things that get rearranged with time & this transient existence interests S. very much. She'd been unusually silent all day long and specially during our English after-supper hour which more or less paralyses her. Every time I looked up (I felt dreary & depressed all day long) her eyes would be on me.

The *Gazette* had horrible things in it: the Afghan woman who was taken as the wife of a Taliban man, raped, branded as a sign of ownership, beaten repeatedly, and insulted & belittled. She had borne a boy in spite of the beatings and was now afraid the father would come back & claim his son. The story of the father who'd burned down the house with his 6 children in it. The story of the mother who drowned her 5 children in the bathtub. Remembering the nurse's aide on Ecstasy who ran into a man who got stuck on her windshield, left him there all night crying for help while she made love with her lover. He died in the course of the night. I'm shut in with these horrible tragedies, including the death of Kierney, the border collie, from epilepsy, ... in *For Love of a Dog*. I think of Gillon, of Monkey, Tidi, Emily and my darling Lily whose tombstone is now visible from my window. But just before I went to bed I read in *Canadian Wildlife* about Mozart and his pet starling. "He helped me with my piano concerto." When the bird died Mozart had a funeral service (like ours with the varied thrush in Vancouver). Suddenly happiness flooded into me. It was another proof of Spinoza's belief that every living animal shares the same nervous system and an identical need to make music and art. My theory that seashells, butterflies, beetles, etc. create themselves or their patterns as squids do in their courting display, and many other animals. The more sophisticated melodies sung by humpback whales from the Indian Ocean. The sharp perfume of the blue hyacinth just behind me—a true cobalt blue. Cynthia will be pleased. "The bird had beautifully revised his *Piano Concerto in G major* ... When the starling died, the musician gave it an elaborate funeral, and later wrote a composition in its honor." I told this to Jovette last night on the phone and she felt instantly happy.

MARCH 19. A *lot* of snow still clinging to the flame tree, big balls on the porch step posts that look so much like snow-covered frozen squirrels that I couldn't believe they weren't until I saw others on Gloria's porch. Our first big snow-storm. Today sky whitish, overcast, big clumps of snow beginning to fall off trees, etc. I feel dizzy with sleepiness.

MARCH 21. This feeling of collapse has been going on for months. Accompanied by wobbliness. 4:30 PM. Snow again. Lise just came for freewriting with Claire—in French? Sleepiness has invaded my brain.

MARCH 23, SATURDAY. Dream—1st scene: *A little boy dressed in shorts down to his knees comes and touches a table like someone coming in from a race. Several times, with a mischievous look on his face. (He looks like the little boy in my Paris sketchbook with a round rosy face.)* 2nd scene: *I'm looking at a landscape and see a statue on top of a man or a woman in robes—bronze. This is the Holy Family, Mary's parents. This comes from* Shadow on the Rock *which I'm reading. Before I notice them a stout man wearing leggings or boots made of heavy pale cloth—a farmer or horseman. He greets me in a friendly way.* This whole dream was elaborate and pleasant with rounded hills and green spring grass ... But another drugged day when my mind works badly & I can't even put the checks in order in my bank statement. I see by my journal that this has been going on for several months.

∾

3/23

Mon très cher Mouser,

Je pense à toi au chaud où tu penses à ta chère Mum à l'humidité printanière de Paris où elle et Monique performent leur noble travail de jury. Moi, je ne sors presque pas. Il y a de la neige jusqu'à mes oreilles et j'ai peur de me perdre. Oh, pourquoi Mum n'est pas capable de dessiner un écureuil. Qu'est-ce que je vais fair comme chat-peintre frustré? ...

Sylvie fait un plat très québécois de morue salée pour le souper. D'abord elle la trempe dans l'eau pour enlever tout le sel avec l'expertise d'Alice B. Toklas. Comme chat qui aime la bonne cuisine je l'admire beaucoup ainsi que celle de Suzanne et Loretta. Il faut dire que ces trois personnes exercent moins de leur génie quand elles font la cuisine pour moi. Les boîtes et de cat-chow spécial tous les jours. Parfois *dear old Mum gives me a piece of her muffin at breakfast. A red-letter day! LOVE and XXX*

❧

03/23/82

Mon très cher Monsen, Je pense à toi au chaud où tu penses à ta chère Mum à l'humidité printanière de Paris où elle et Monique performent leur noble travail de jury. Moi, je ne sors presque pas. Il y a de la neige jusqu'à mes oreilles et j'ai peur de me perdre. Oh, pourquoi Mum n'est pas capable de dessiner un écureuil. Qu'est-ce que je vais faire comme chat-peintre frustré? Évidemment ta ta Mum l'as convaincu m'a que c'est possible d'envoyer un fax à l'hôtel avec le nom bizarre. On va voir. Tu sais que je suis un peu shamanesse et sais quand c'est l'heure pour mon nouveau cat-chow. Sylvie fait un plat très québécois de morue salée pour le souper. D'abord elle la trempe dans l'eau pour enlever tout le sel avec l'expertise d'Alice B. Toklas. Comme chat qui aime la bonne cuisine je l'admire beaucoup ainsi que celle de Suzanne et Loretta. Il faut dire que ces trois personnes exercent moins de leur génie quand elles font la cuisine pour moi. Les boîtes et de cat-chow spécial tous les jours. Parfois dear old Mum gives me a piece of her muffin at breakfast. A red-letter day! LOVE and XXX to you, cher Monsen et à ta Mum et à Monique

SUNDAY MARCH 24. Palm Sunday and the snow is deep in the garden, the weeping juniper is forlornly bent over and black & perhaps dead. My usual pessimism & depression. Where was I last March? Did I gaze out the window longingly everyday? Did March seem to go on forever? But nothing died, everything turned green in the glorious spring. Did therapy at the Royal Vic make March seem less awful? The time before melting—I missed most of it here at my window where the little dramas of death and revival and another death played themselves out. And I wasn't quite as conscious of the sleepy syndrome that kills all energy and makes me feel constantly wobbly & my brain uncertain. This morning I could hardly stand on my left foot. Now it's O.K. again.

In my dreams *there are very kind women, simply dressed and rather nunnish who pass and exchange friendly words as if they've known me for a long time.* I fall asleep right away after bedpan, somewhat surprised to see it's gone, in the warm covers, in rather uncomfortable positions and sleep for a little while, and have my usual illusions about an energetic day coming up until my left leg refuses to obey me. Now I'm slouched on my chair with my eyes closed.

MARCH 25. Mike stepped on the control for the bed this morning early and it tipped me high and slid me down so that my feet ran into the foot of the bed. It always feels as though I'm swaddled tight with bedclothes and can't move in any direction. 6 AM. Leonie has gone into the dining room, I want to pee. I call her, it seems loudly, perhaps five times. She finally comes with a stony face, brings bedpan, gets me up exactly at 6:30, still in her implacable, jerky, slightly careless state. Much affectionate patting on the shoulder before she leaves & post-check.

MARCH 26. More snow announced for this afternoon. *A lot*—15–20 cm. Limpness & depression. Claire—we're discussing paranoia. I talk about article about mustard gas & say I imagine it's in the air, poisoning us all in minute doses. I say we'll wear buttons saying "I belong to Paranoids Anonymous. Join!" She said she was already, that everybody is tired and that that's winter. I must tell her about the smell of apples—and Hertel's mustard gas. Miky sits like a statue (he's sitting motionless with his back turned now—are his eyes glazed?) He just turned his head and looked out the window with a keen look. Like a lioness with light-filled eyes. Licking his paws with back turned. I feel sad for my weeping spruce & rhododendron.

Dream: *I'm looking at a book about as thin as this journal with nice handmade-looking paper like this. It's called* Il Inflagrante. *I repeated it to myself several times when I woke up and probably got it wrong anyway. It seemed to be full of meaning about wrong-doing. It was an old classic that I'd been meaning to read for years* ... Mike is lying partly on my notebook now—a victory that he's been pushing for all morning. Paw quite yellow at beginning of leg with widely spaced black stripes, the last vestiges of tiger. Encroaching.

MARCH 28. A spring day? Persistent snow covering Gloria's frog & bowing over the weeping juniper. Rhododendron not visible. No part of me seemed to work this morning. Eyes bad, walking cautious & wobbly.

MARCH 31. Easter Day. Cloudless, sunny, v. light wind? Thermometer around 7° ... The conifers are miraculously turning green; the weeping juniper is straightening up a dark green now—my dear little tree, & the small spruce on the right is splendid ... A nice talk with Maureen[55] this morning—about 9/11, the groups immediately set up, ways to help people, to comfort them, to search for them. The massage therapy for both people and dogs, who walked over the hot fragments of the buildings and burned their feet ... A policeman; his gun was found, bent, and a grave made at that spot. Maureen joined a writing workshop in October in old St. Paul's Church which was close to the Twin Towers & miraculously untouched—to exchange experiences and reactions, fears & losses. I love Maureen's slow, flat voice that rolls along as if it carries the entire story intact, with her half-smile in it even when it's very serious ...

APRIL 5, THURSDAY. Big interval since I last wrote. Yesterday Verena & I did freewriting from Bill Merwin. The first one "Now all my teachers are dead except silence" and we both did good ones somewhat similar ... A little later Cynthia called me to say she was going to have a biopsy for something suspicious in her breast. I had a nervous tremor and I spoke only gibberish, in spite of determined efforts to say words. I recognized this as a "floater" (?) one of the small strokes that can hit you at any time. Cynthia said, "I'll call you tomorrow morning." I had a sort of subdued headache but my speech came back after about 1/2 hour when I'd brushed my teeth & sat down in my chair & was just sitting with my eyes closed. V. had left for the Blue Metropolis. Night O.K. Mike woke me up insistently again today at 5:45

55. Maureen Brady.

& I ended by pushing him off. Later when I got up he was sitting quietly with his front paws curled inward in front of him. Now I feel uncertain, careful about writing without making mistakes.

APRIL 6. Yesterday—with Verena. An abject depression. I kept saying things that would instantly close a trap on me ...

⌘

April 10

Dear Mouser—what felicity, you and your Mum are together again and you can be happy and eat Fancy Feast and other delicacies and spring will come up here. In fact, Mum has been looking out and seeing patches of green where the yew and juniper trees are peeping through the balcony railings. I had to laugh this morning when Mum tipped the walker forward with everything in it and then picked everything up with the reacher. Now it's 2 PM and Suzanne has just come in with groceries and Mum & I have been sitting on her bed & old Mum has been nice to me as befits someone of my supreme charm—imagine preferring that hirsute animal Lily to me, cat-goddess rest her soul. Well, I'm going out on the back porch with Mum to look for signs of spring and then Suzanne (I ♥ Suzanne) is going to wash Mum's hair and it's about time if you ask me.

XXXX to you and your Mummy—

⌘

APRIL 16, TUESDAY. A big leap without writing. Ups and downs of depression. States of collapse, high blood pressure with people coming ... Spring suddenly quietly speaking its sign—silence. The magical greening, a crocus in front & several now, it seems, in back & scyllas. (Sweet-smelling blue hyacinths from Cynthia & daffodils from Yvonne.) The yew very green & the sturdy little Alberto spruce swelling into a small cloud. A faint sun persistently dispelling the fog. Invisible but announced. Like my effort to concentrate to put words together intelligibly—a kind of pushing. The sun just broke through not as sunshine and shadow, no shadow, just light. Yes, a soft shadow on the fence marks the back of the house.

APRIL 17. Sitting at my table—a drop falls out of my mouth. A pale sky & sunshine. Temp. climbing up to 28° C. Still wearing my old checked P-town jacket. Last night Suzanne & I had supper on the porch—lovely. She had put out the little fountain and Vogel's statue—very dark red and golden yellow (I long for this to turn grey like the fence across the way). At the far end of the garden a clump of scyllas and some pale crocuses. All conifers nice and green, blue-green, yellow-green. For some reason I expected to feel more energetic today ... & I felt as limp as ever. M. Carol brought me a photograph of her beautiful, long-haired orange cat to show me and said, "She's a lesbian." "How do you know?" I asked. "She told me." She had her spayed and changed her name to Billy Jean, B.J. for short. Beautiful.

❧

April 21

Most dear Mouser,

Mum just decided to call you & your dear Mum and I think got the wrong number. She & I are in a state of gloom (GLOOM) because the temperature went down to -3° last night and Mum doesn't have the courage to see if the pot of beautiful thriving basil survived or is kaput.

Mum is sad because her friends at Bryn Mawr keep dying. Yesterday dear old Mike Nicolls called and said Betsy Harvey who had a lot of sadness in her life already, died. When she was in her 70's or 80's she developed a new method of making photographs, sort of surrealist & had shows. Mike sounded quite peppy. She and Mum and I agree that old age is the pits. Not for weaklings, said some witty woman.

Sylvie just came in bearing the moribund basil. Mum says always follow your instincts even if it means letting me Mike slip out into the cold ...

Love and XXX from

M & MM

❧

Sunday April 21, '02

Most dear Mouser,

Mum just decided to call you & your dear Mum and I think got the wrong number – She & I are in a state & gloom (GLOOM) because the temperature went down to -3° last night and Mum doesn't have the courage to see if the pot & beautiful·thriving basil survived or is kaput–

Mum is sad because her friends at Bryn Mawr keep dying – Yesterday dear old Mike Nicolls called and said Betsy Harvey who had a lot of sadness in her life already, died – When she was in her 70's or 80's she developed a new method of making photographs, sort & surrealist & had shows – Mike sounded quite peppy – She and Mum and I agree that old age is the pits – Not for weaklings, said some witty woman.

Sylvie just came in bearing the moribund basil – Mum says always follow your instincts even if it means letting me Mike slip out into the cold –

Mum & I got your schedule all mixed up – You, dear Mouser are being vaccinated May 6th? It sounds like a prudent project what with all the the beefed-up border cats – Love and XXX from

M & MM

My dear Mouser—Mme. L'Espérance really outdid herself and your Mum spoiled my old Mum (what is so remarkable about getting to the age of 85, I'd like to know. Parrots can do it just as well as that and can sing, too—)

Mum is waiting for Dr.? who is coming today to see if he wants to take her on as a patient. He sounds very nice on the telephone.

He was very nice and very interested in Mum's painting & bone carving (he, too, has worked with bones) and his wife wrote a book called The Archaeology of Madness. Alas, he is allergic to CATS and what a shock when I, Mike, was put out in the cold by Verena and I beat angrily on the door while Dr. K. talked & talked with Mum and Verena. Now I'm inside & have been soothed with loving words. Mouser that cow Mum just drew is just TERRIBLE. How can those kind-hearted people Verena & Lise think she can write a book. The poor old person has lost her marbles & I saw it long ago.

XXXXX

MAY 6. My eyes feel terrible. Rain, just as Verena was preparing to work outside ... 3 PM. The mute sky, almost white, but maple buds burst against it. My state reminds me of the oiled bird image in my freewriting. The temptation to rub my right eye. V. just came in with geraniums, scarlet and white, a new kind, she says, in no way resembles a geranium, snapdragons, daisies, from Atwater Market ... The yew is sending out its little yellow sprouts, clematis coming up, the small Alberta spruce a dense green globe, peonies a foot high.

May 7
... That pesky squirrel keeps on perfecting his act in a most insolent way ...

MAY 8. Cloudless, it seems, greener and greener. Mike came to wake me up & act as a sentinel, pushed comfortably against me with his head held high and eyes wide open. Silent, serious, front paws folded in. He's in that position now on the Armenian rug. I woke up early again, and had to pee repeatedly. Eliz. very patient and nice. Have yielded to the temptation to rub stuff out of my right eye ... Not helpful.

The spring green of the flame tree against shadowy dark of brick garage wall behind ... The need to close my eyes. Mike just went to the front door to greet Suzanne. She picks him up and holds him facing her, with his paws around her neck while she utters soothing sounds. Faint cirrus clouds spreading down the blue sky in long almost invisible veils.

MAY 9. A day just as Eliz. predicted: cool (12°), grey—colorless, windy. Rain later. My eyes prickle & itch & I walk cautiously ... Have done nothing positive except read this journal which in its subdued way is more interesting than I thought it would be ...

MAY 10. Bunches of new leaves shadow-boxing against the sunlit brick wall in gusts of wind.

MAY 11, SATURDAY. Windy again but not like yesterday with its furious gusts. Today a shadow chases over the bowl of the fountain ... Claire just called, anxious in her usual bountiful way, to "bring something"—anything. "I cannot come empty-handed," she says. Me: "Why not. Other people do!" This sounds spoiled and ungrateful for simple visits. Of course, one brings "something" as a kind of shield, a diversion from the unworthiness of the inadequate self—and it grows into a grand competition.

MAY 12, SUNDAY. Still, colorless, dispirited day and *cold*. Reminds me of Verena's "and *breathe*." I hate to be reminded of something so elementary but it's true one can forget. Or perhaps I'm practicing for an amphibious life. A return after a long absence.

∽

Dear Mouser—you must have at least 20 lives unlike run-of-the mill cats (I am not one of them, as you know) but it's terrible that you have to waste them on those terrible pills. What a menace and self-sacrifice to go to Canada, who would have thought it? But you will like seeing Sammy-boy— when is he coming? and your favorite haunts, and mine too. Oh how well I know every mole-tunnel and skunk burrow. Though we must try to be nice to our fellow creatures, don't you think, specially those darling little snakes that shed their lovely silvery skins. My mum says she was a 3-toed sloth asleep on a treetop in a previous life. She did everything very slowly she says; it took about a day to get down to the bottom of the tree. Everything is so green here but it's cold. How can that be when you are limp from the heat?

I imagine winds fighting it out somewhere between Key West and Montreal. Verena did some planting—some scarlet geraniums that dazzle my old eyes. Mum & I don't have much to say. On Monday Suzanne will bring us a book about elephants painting. It seems they all like to get together and paint like crazy in a sanctuary. So you see some good things are happening in this woe-filled world dear Mouser. And you've recovered.

   Much love & kisses

~

Sunday May 12, 2002

Dear Mouser – You must have at least 20 lives unlike run-of-the-mill cats (I am not one of them, as you know) but it's terrible that you have to waste them in those terrible pills. What a menace and self-sacrifice to go to Canada, who would have thought it? But you will like seeing Sammy-boy – when is he coming? and your favourite haunts, and mine, too. Oh how well I know every mole, tunnel and skunk burrow. Though we must try to be nice to our fellow creatures, don't you think, specially those darling little snakes that shed their lovely silvery skins.

My mum says she was a 3-toed sloth asleep on a tree – very top in a previous life. She did everything very slowly she says. ZZZZ it took about a day to get down to the bottom of the tree.

Everything is so green here but it'll cold. How can that be when you are limp from the heat? I imagine winds fighting it out

Somewhere between Key West and Montreal – Verena did some planting – some scarlet geraniums that dazzle my old eyes – Mum & I don't have much to say. On Monday Suzanne will bring us a book about elephants painting. It seems they all like to get together and paint like crazy in a sanctuary. So you see some good things are happening in this woe-filled world dear Mouser. And you've recovered. Much love & kisses from me Mike and

MUM WAKE UP!

MAY 13. My hands are cold, the smoke detector keeps making little plaintive whistles. More urgent just now. A death-whistle. This morning I woke up around 5, couldn't sleep, began to think about extermination of fish, complete disruption of the ocean's chain of life, up to the great whales. The fishermen pulling in almost empty nets except for starving dolphins caught in them. The pollution of more & more shorelines with fish farms. And people happily forking mouthfuls of swordfish and halibut, the last ones, that cost $50 a serving, into their mouths. Bushmeat in Africa, too. There is none left. I fell asleep in my chair and woke up suddenly when I toppled sideways and just retrieved myself in time ...

The petty indignities of old age.[56] She is in the third person. She is presumed to be deaf. She has a hearing-aid but it doesn't work with the telephone. "Excuse me just a second," she says. "I have to take my hearing-aid out." This doesn't make sense and by the time she has taken out the hearing-aid which looks like a naked new-born possum, turned off its squeak and put it in a safe place, the person on the phone has hung up. She begins the day feeling stupid—a chronic state ...

A. has come to look over business mail, make out checks to sign. "Where is?" she asks. "What happened to?" She doesn't drum her fingers on the table but exaggerated terror and fear suffuse M. Impatience, invisible as air, instantly detectable—M. crumples up. She doesn't know where she put? "Look at me," says A. sharply. M. jerks her head up and looks at her. Student control, she thinks. The old person becomes a person who can be disciplined. Lesson—you must learn to have the dignity of someone who can't be disciplined. Resentment is a cowardly emotion, the admission of power. Resentment outlives speech. It has its own wordless memory once its story gets worn out in the telling. See Blake's *Poison Tree* in the *Songs of Experience*.

MAY 14. In old age I sit and brood. My friends make touching efforts to make me happy. But the old happiness, the kind that took over my entire body and which I can remember from childhood, has no energy and doesn't last long, hardly survives the day, has a hint of doubt in it. The chickadees, their sudden appearance that made me truly happy, has turned to anxiety. Why don't they come? Is it too cold? Were they bothered by the appearance of the squirrel? Were they eaten by the crow Sylvie and I saw? Are the sunflower seeds mouldy from all the rain? Today is cold and windy with fitful periods of sunshine—some slippery stuff to keep the squirrels from climbing. So now I worry about the squirrel. Has he fallen off and hurt himself? His

56. On looseleaf paper, dated May 13.

ballet performance between post and feeder beautiful to see, hanging on with his back paws, fully stretched out to grasp the feeder and extract a sunflower seed with a front paw & delicate claw. I heard a thump this morning—was it our squirrel sliding off the post and falling? Getting anywhere fast is impossible so I don't even try. But always imagine the worst. This pessimism has gotten to be pathological; I have to make a big effort to keep it from bursting out of my mouth. The exercise of a twisted kind of power: *Cogito ergo sum.* Optimism seems to me less genuine, a sort of disguise or papering-over. Cassandra was always right, wasn't she? Marie-Claire seems to say that there is a redeeming beauty in every tragedy, such as the story of Jessica, the 11-year-old pilot. A kind of optimism?

Later, 11:15. Suzanne came. The chickadees came. The squirrel came. The other face of pessimism. S. hadn't put any slippery stuff on the post and we agreed that we didn't want to. So I felt happy, saved from myself. Old selves are in danger of themselves. It seems to require a certain kind of health, the feeling of conviviality, no envy of people's ability to move—like Nawrie in Scotland with David. The hoof and mouth menace ended, the smell of death gone. The bird walkers free to walk.

MAY 17, FRIDAY. COLD still. 8°, perhaps. A frost tonight. Overcast but glimpses of blue sky. Overcome by sleepiness. Dream—just before waking up, 6:40. *I am in an old train station in England waiting for my train. It is built with very small-hewn blocks of granite blackened by soot (about 2" by 2"). I get on the 1st train that comes and decide to go past the first station, then realize that I've come too far and have to get off. The people I try to talk to speak a foreign language (Chinese?) but finally I meet an English woman, old (75?) wearing a flannel darkish suit, with her frizzy grey hair, hair pulled back in a bun. She, too, is looking for the train that goes back to the first station. We walk quite fast over rough hard bare ground, rocky, and pass a door made of small stones with an oval opening in it. My friend opens it, looks in, says, "Oh no!" withdraws and we go on walking. I think, perhaps, it was the toilet.* I wake up wanting to pee and see that I'm late getting up (It's 6:40). I get up and ache all over and can barely make it to the bathroom. The dream seems to be about my actual fear of lateness and anxiety ...

SUNDAY, MAY 19. The pink flowering fruit tree towering higher than the garage, breaks through the bright green of Gloria's maple tree, trying to hide it—a more visible brightness but less powerful. Ann just called, back from

Maine. Stormy weather; I can call up the smell of ocean water and see waves breaking on the long beach. Bad nostalgia ...

MAY 23. Leaf shadows shivering in the wind.

MAY 29. Supper on the porch last night. As the sun was setting somewhere behind us, the white suet among dark leaves was illuminated like a piece of alabaster.

MAY 30. 2 dreams. *In the first I meet with Dr. K. who smiles at me in a wonderfully kindly way. She says, still smiling, "You're riddled with cancer." This doesn't fill me with despair, rather, a kind of resignation. In the second dream I am standing at the edge of a huge crater made of pale dry, rough sand. I have two red buttons in my hand, about as big as dimes. I throw one in ... (Or do I somehow let it fall in?) It lands about 15 feet from the top rim and I know that if I climb down to get it I'll fall down and roll to the bottom. I stand there waiting for help in a state of great anxiety and wake up.* Miky has been trying to wake me up by walking over my stomach.

MAY 31. Damp after rain last night, rain, thunderstorms, wind predicted. Curtain of green in garden, a dense, country landscape, lilac blossoms cautiously opening & sweet smell of lilies-of-the-valley. Miky in his guardian role this morning. 5:45–6:30—he pushes close, lies with his front paws straight out, head lifted and gazing straight ahead. Vigilantly. Immovable. At 6:30 I had to gently push him away to get out of bed ...

Dream: *I'm in a big workroom with rooms but no doors looking for the designer of the furniture (unfinished) inside. I see him but he seems to move away from me, to avoid me. Finally I catch up to him and say that I'd like to buy the little low table shaped like a half-moon. He says it isn't good enough, he hasn't finished it, etc. I say, "It will be a melting pot." This seems wonderfully appropriate to me. I smile at everybody in a self-satisfied way (there are other people around now; in the beginning I've been alone).* I'm talking about my house and the things in it.

Anna's[57] letter yesterday & the two dreams about Annie. Her saying in one of them that she was walking to Canada to see me. A warm happiness.

57. Annie Poor's niece.

JUNE 3, MONDAY. Dream. *I'm on a film set somewhere in the country. I walk by a pile of rather muddy compost. There is the flattened skin of a red fox lying on top of it without a head. This is one of two in the dream, I'd already picked up the other but there was no sign of it. It, too, was headless; they were cured but rather stiff with thin fur ...*

JUNE 4. Brilliant sunshine & blue sky. Cool—17°? I'm full of piercing nostalgia after writing Anna about her dreams and the birds singing in the early morning quiet of Memorial Day in Boston. Death of my friends and of Sarah and the death of birdsong—particularly, that of the most familiar bird of all, a robin.

JUNE 14, FRIDAY. Various friends (Jovette?) have reported seeing flocks of robins. To woo one into this garden ... I usually hear them in the street. 10 days of *not* writing in my journal. Why? A continuous stupor—inability to think. I must write down fragments. Yesterday when I fell down I was already leaning over with the plastic box full of chow. I pulled the walker over with me, the tray detached itself and the contents spilled over the far side of the kitchen. It was impossible to reach for anything when I was lying on my back so first I pushed the Lifeline button. Beep, beep, beep beep, "Miss Meigs! Are you alright?" I said I'd just fallen down in the kitchen. Silence for about 1/2 hr. and I pushed the button repeatedly. Silence. Slight panic. Then Yvonne & Jessie showed up & hauled me up (I'd already slid or heaved myself so I was leaning against the kitchen table.) My tailbone hurt but not very much. Left shoe was coming off, glasses were lying on far side of kitchen. I'd gotten hold of reacher without toppling over & dragged walker tray toward me. Empty, of course. From Lifelines' point of view they'd done a very good job, from mine they'd caused me unnecessary anxiety. Yvonne said she'd thought they wanted to come & clean the carpets & had said, "No thanks." She hadn't had breakfast or gotten dressed. Anyway she stayed on here, sitting on my bed with a kindly watchful look, until Suzanne came.

JUNE 23. St. Jean Baptiste—damp, warm the tail end of a dream. *I'm being driven by an unknown friendly man in an open touring car. We go up a grassy hill without a road or an opening in a long hedge—like the row of spruce trees at Sims Rd. He stops. I wave my hand at an opening. He says, "Well you're a clever little lady." He turns and drives through the opening and I feel very pleased and satisfied with myself.* I've had several dreams lately where these bland, pleasant men turn up—wearing tweed suits and golf caps like father's, (I feel as though I'm in the act of inventing this) but pale, with a checked pattern, not a uniform tweedy-smelling brown.

Today a warm pale-blue haze over everything. My inability to think ... My friends are leaving and coming back ... And I'm struggling with my preface, all in inept pieces ...

JULY 7. Not quite so desperately sleepy today but unbalanced. Slowly clearing. The pink roses ... A cluster and then 4 separate ones against dark blue-green leaves. Then interval to the slightly pinky orange of tiger daylilies, more beautiful than the ones at Sims Road, turned toward the sun away from house ... The ones here (and the pink roses) are almost straight up, toward the invisible sun. The perennial bachelors' buttons on this side of Lily's tombstone are so lacy & blue I can't even see them. Delphinium, a straight spine turning from white to pale blue.

Bad crankiness and forgetfulness lately. With Eleanor and Sherry I forgot the whole of the article about *Documenta*, what big shows had become. Tried to invent something and began to stammer. A sense of them patient, intelligently with amusement, waiting for me to say something that made sense. The nightmare of losing the power of speech. Hoarse voice. And going over my old drawings I can't remember when I did them or sometimes where. Was it in Maine or Wellfleet? Apple trees? Do they have leaves? Blossoms? Truro? One, that looks like a woman's torso, seems to be an olive tree but there is only one ... Sylvie brought down another pile for today— more pine trees on dunes ... perhaps one good in five ... the heavy dragging-down of myself—every aspect—by myself. When Beth said, "You're beautiful," the other day I could only look dumbly into space

JULY 20, SATURDAY. Cloudless, 16°, windy. No clematis buds, no pink rosebuds.

～

Très cher Mouser et sa carissima mamma.

Ton *fax after prolonged labor ... delivered a very nice fax and then a twin (identical). My mum was starting this and lo and behold Verena appeared looking as blue-eyed as you (maybe she was a Siamese cat in a former life and you knew each other). She and Lise M. had been to L'Isle Verte and Bic, the dernier cri of places to go except for us cats these days. I've told Mum that she is turning into an envious old croak; it's unseemly when one* considers the islands, mountains, beaches, birds in her long life. I weep for her sunny disposition.

Yesterday a not very big long-haired black cat with wild desperate look came through the garden crying. I felt so sorry for a brother cat but he refused to stay. Mum's heart was broken again (it breaks every day so not to worry. It self-mends) ...

LOVE

FROM MIKE-   TO MOOSER-
                20 juillet 2002

Très cher Mooser et sa carissima mamma. Ton fax after prolonged labor... 21 juillet delivered a very nice fax and then a twin (identical) My Mum was starting this and loandbehold Verena appeared looking as blue-eyed as you (maybe she was a Siamese cat in a former life and you knew each other) She and Lise had been to L'Isle Verte and Bic, the dernier cri &places to go except for us cats these days. I've told Mum that she is turning into an envious old CROAK; it's unseemly when one considers the islands, mountains, beaches, birds in her long life. I weep for her sunny disposition.

Yesterday a not very big long-haired black cat with wild desperate look came through the garden crying. I felt so sorry for a brother cat but he refused to stay. Mum's heart was broken again (it breaks every day so not to worry. It self-mends.) Well, everybody has gotten married and now Mary Meigs is Mary Thorne which is weird when you come to think of it and Phoebe is Phoebe Strand. Personally I like to be Mike Period, race parisienne, dating from First Tigers. Mum sends love to your Tante Michèle, Tante Pauline, Tante Hélène and all your many admirers including your dear dear Mum-
                                    L O V E

JULY 30. Clematis flowering! 2 flowers. A few tiny apples on Dolgo ...

AUGUST 1, THURSDAY. Dream. *I'm looking at a map of Spain, a roadmap. Friends are starting today to drive north through a dense network of roads which I trace tentatively with my finger. I'm resigned to the fact that I can't go.*

Thoughts about old age—from reading *Unless* which seems to be in the language of Carol Shields' struggle against breast cancer—her pain particularly. Her humor, idle, finely observant, is almost like a medication—morphine?—that eases the pain and sharpens her incredible watchfulness, even what she sees out of the corner of her eye without seeming to stare. I suddenly fell in love with the book. Maybe it was simply the sentence, "Gwen had come out as a lesbian," dropped casually and unreferred to so far—30 pp. later. I love her conversational habit of leaving a subject in midair ...

Last night I called Margaret S. She had fallen down and cracked the last vertebra but felt no pain for several days and suddenly excruciating pain ... She uses the kind of walker that has a seat to get around. "Old age is just awful, isn't it?" she said & I agreed heartily. In old age we are forced to speak a foreign language, we are people who are forbidden to speak our mother tongue. The process of deterioration is made easy for us by memory loss, the accidental breaking of bones, the dimming of eyes; each body selects its own way of inflicting damage, willy-nilly ... Memory like plasma or a blood transfusion restores the tissue around it.

Yesterday S. found my poems ... dozens of ones I'd forgotten. They brought back periods of time, portraits—black & white Minnie, for instance the barn swallows & bobolinks & whippoorwill, the rich life of animals and birds at Baker Road. Darling Emily when we drove to the kennels for the last time and she said goodbye to me in the jeep. I was filled with a deep sense of reliving my life with my animal friends and of our importance to each other. Today my joy in finding a precise past is spoiled by "the deep silt of guilt" (I say in a poem, for there were poems, too, that I'd forgotten, about old age when I was only 59, and yet I claim now *never to have felt old*.) Nearly 30 years ago I was mulling over how I would die, would I "complain and complain," would I "remember to love" and now I think, is everybody as self-centered? Carol Shields isn't. About my dogs and cats, too. I betrayed them, turned them over to someone else to be euthanized. I don't even remember how Gracie died and there is no one to ask. List: Gracie, Sam, Gillon, Emily, Emma, Winky, Frimousse, Sheila, (Polly and Chanel and

Molly who were in my care only briefly). Cats: Minny, Lulu, Pitty, Tidi, Tido, Lily Briscoe & 4 kittens: Agnes Grey, Toby, Mike, Lily.

August 3, Saturday. Overwhelming temptation to scratch my itchy right eye, worse than left eye. Cloudless day ... A feeling in both my ears as though they are being pulled ... Old age, self-hate an acid contempt ...

3 Août '02 samedi

Très cher Mouser — Merci pour ton beau fax de hier — J'aime beaucoup tes auto-portraits et les glears and it all makes me think of yesteryear as I curl up on the cool floor and dream for several hours of cats — Mum made a list of all the cats she and your Mum and Bobbie had had and then of all the dogs — She couldn't remember the lamented Minny's name, he just disappeared and never came back, didn't he? So many gone as Dante said so poetically, thinking about his favorite cats and dogs. Do you think Dante's favorite cat looked like me? or heaven forbid like Lily?

Sylvie just came wearing the most beautiful red Thai silk skirt almost to her ankles — I think I'd look nice in one but I don't want to compromise my male dignity — Oh yes & Mum has been thinking about whip-poor-wills, too, the poor old person, living in memories of birds & dogs & cats that inspired poems she's forgotten having written & Suzanne just found. Plus she thinks about your cardinals — I hope if I were there I'd just gaze at them admiringly and not be tempted to • you know what, part of my youthful folly — Goodbye from me, Mike

with kisses & hugs to your mum & you from you

∾

Très cher Mouser—Merci pour ton beau fax d'hier. J'aime beaucoup tes auto-portraits et les fleurs *and it all makes me think of yesteryear as I curl up on the cool floor and dream for several hours of cats. Mum made a list of all the cats she and your mum and Bobbie had had and then of all the dogs. She couldn't remember the lamented Minny's name, he just disappeared and never came back, didn't he? So many gone as Dante said so poetically, thinking about his favorite cats and dogs. Do you think Dante's favorite cat looked like me? or heaven forbid like Lily?*

Sylvie just came wearing the most beautiful red Thai silk skirt almost to her ankles. I think I'd look nice in one but I don't want to compromise my male dignity. Oh yes ⊄ Mum has been thinking about whip-poor-wills, too, the poor old person, living in memories of birds ⊄ dogs ⊄ cats that inspired poems she'd forgotten having written ⊄ Suzanne just found. Plus she thinks about your cardinals. I hope if I were there I'd just gaze at them admiringly and not be tempted to you know what, part of my youthful folly.

Goodbye from me, Mike

∾

AUGUST 4. Hot, sunshine slowly pushing through blue haze. 30° predicted later but showers predicted for this evening and tomorrow ... The poignant sadness in dogs' eyes. I keep a newspaper clipping of Squeak, the Jack Russell terrier who went to the funeral service of his master in Zimbabwe and refused to leave his body when he was executed.

Yesterday I felt joyful when Sylvie brought 3 books about gardens, brick walks and patios from the library, including one about Sissinghurst. So enthusiastic about replacing the cement slabs with old bricks and planting lots more flowers—perennials: roses, delphiniums, hollyhocks, echinacea, daisies, Iceland poppies. More portulaca next spring. Columbine for round bed.

Dream. *I go out of a narrow door in a house without windows to a wide view of a glassily calm sea that tips toward me. I see two whales swimming toward me in the transparent green water. They are long and slender and shiny black, about the size of minke whales, and have small white teeth the length of their jaws. The one closest to me sees me and turns a little to swim straight toward me. I seem to be both in the water and watching from shore and am not at all afraid. The landscape—calm water and mild sunshine—is very beautiful and I feel happy when I wake up.* Now I've fallen into the state of sleepiness that paralyses me, unsteady on my feet, hardly able to think, slightly nauseated, but the whales take me back to an old dream-state with poetic meaning and images. Was it my joy about the idea of a path made of old bricks?

AUGUST 5, 10 AM. An awful smell coming up from the cellar. Miky went down & is probably there on the cool floor. I feel so sad as his hair gets more and more matted and he is always hungry and thirsty & opens his mouth in almost silent cries (my ears, probably) ... Dream last night, all women this time, no one I know. *I appear before each one and every time I make a little dance step, an entrechat a kind of propitiation.* Maybe this comes from the little bows Suzanne makes when I thank her for something. A small ceremony.

AUGUST 6. Pink rose more & more beautiful. Diane[58] brought digital photos of me (hadn't remembered!) really nice. The colors are beautiful.

I've been thinking about how destructive senility can be, how it can change people's characters from gentle to violent & abusive ... In myself I notice gratuitous spitefulness—which *has* always been there—doesn't qualify for Carol Shields' *goodness* without vengeance. Vengeance, like Hertel with the sweet smell of apples that have been sprayed 19 times, and contain a residue of poison.

AUGUST 8. Dream. All I can remember is the part about Sarah looking at me. *Her eyes were a clear transparent blue like water. I thought they were really green and yet it was Sarah ...*

∽

Care Mouser e sua cara mam(m)a—I'm trying to stay cool under Mum's bed. Mum has a new malady: spelling-loss. She can't remember if it's mamma or mama, seive or sieve and the mighty English languish (you see what I mean?) is now a millstone around her neck. Have you heard about the big brown cloud 40 km. deep? How about its significance for us cats and catamarans? Mom showed me some Ogden Nash poems in the New Yorker *& I could hardly have done better myself (Mum has been keeping my poems in a secret place in the event of some unavoidable eventuality. At which point they will be dug up and a book will be written* Why Cats Write Poems *and we will all have a Day of Rejoicing ...)*

Goodbye dear Mouser, I'm afraid Mum has lost a few more marbles.

Much love from me Mike &

∽

58. Diane Trépanière, photographer, also occasional caretaker.

Monday August 12, '02

Cara Monser and .... e sua cara
mam̃ma .... I'm trying to
stay cool and .... Mum's bed.
Mum has a new .... malady: spelling-loss.
She can't remember if it's mamma or mama, sieve or
sieve and the mighty English language (you see what I
mean?) is now a millstone around her neck.
Have you heard about
the big brown cloud
40 km. deep? How about its significance
for us cats and catamarans? Mum
showed me some Ogden Nash poems in The New Yorker
& I could hardly have done better myself (Mum has
been keeping my poems in a secret place in the event
of some unavoidable eventuality. At which point
they will be dug up and a book will be written Why
Cats write Poems
and we will all have
a Day of Rejoicing
& will by President
G. W. Bush who I'm
sorry to say has a chat parisien that he rescued
from an alley in back of the White House. where he
had gone to pray for the destruction of evil.

Goodbye dear Monser,   miaow!
I'm afraid Mum has
lost a few more marbles
        Much love
            from me Mike &

            Canelle   comes with
                      Suzanne B.

AUGUST 14. Hateful heat and drought going on and on; no promise of rain, just "a possible thunderstorm" that hasn't yet materialized ... Early this morning I began thinking about Aunt Bessie and the Wurts family. Aunt Bessie's parties with their raucous laughter. Aunt B.'s biting words to me, "Why don't you get married? You're just an ordinary American girl." As bad as Eliz. Smart's "polite vomit." The two poles of mediocrity or perhaps the same. Then I dreamt that I was talking to Margaret Atwood. She was telling me where she went to go swimming, speaking with flat enthusiasm and half-smile.

Cynthia in bad pain, took a pill while she was here. Her face sunburned but tense, drawn ... She said there's no further operation beyond these two possible. She goes swimming in her little lake. She described how the loon jumped on the merganser who had dared to raise a family on the lake and that they hadn't come back this year. "The loons have taken over the lake." She described the battle, how huge the loon had looked punishing the merganser ...

11 AM I just called Alice[59] who seems fairly well. Has trouble with her hearing-aid just like mine. Says Joe will bring her to see me.

SATURDAY, AUGUST 17. Sunny, no sign of rain or thunderstorm. This is the third day, "possibility of a thunderstorm, 60% chance of rain." A new malady, weather-rage. Eyes bad again, as though pieces of dust were just inside eyelids. Vision bad. I see things. My eyes see lies, shadows of cats, Mike's shadows, the repertoire ...

AUGUST 18. The heat and smog goes on. High blood pressure, systolic and pulse last night. Sylvie suggested I call the CLSC and I balked. At noon Alma, Cynthia Lynn, friend from England with a name like Persimmon (forgotten) came with lunch. Turbot cooked with onions and ginger, guacamole which I devoured despite my boycott and longed for more. Cindy very shy. I kept asking drawing-out questions that sounded stupid to me, followed by short answers & long silences. Cindy's partner is a gay man, P. is in love with a man. I talked lamely about the advantages of having a man in your life. Hypocrite! ...

This morning I read over my lighthearted journal from CHUS. Even though my left side works much better now—i.e. left hand (small movements) and foot—knee still locks, walking is persistently wobbly & I'm totally dependent on the walker, speech is more blurred (so are eyes) memory is worse, I don't dare go down porch steps (and Verena said not to) and I am *sleepier* every day (because of high blood pressure medication?).

SATURDAY, AUGUST 24. A small cluster of reddening Dolgo apples, alone on the tree. Squirrels have reappeared, their tails scrawny. Why? Miky's fur is

---

59. Alice Diabo, one of the old women on the bus in *The Company of Strangers*. Alice died just weeks before Mary.

getting tufty. But he came to wake me up this morning and lay quietly by my side. Yesterday I saw him leap nimbly over the fence to join Gloria's grey cat who raced to Gloria's, looking somewhat dishevelled from G.'s garden, and into G.'s open door. Proof that catfriends are more important than human ...

Reading Emily Carr, *The Heart of a Peacock*. These are short stories illustrated by her and not at all what I expected, i.e. studies of animal behavior ... Present in all the books—her rage against human meanness of spirit and smallness of mind, a surprising vanity in the Emily character when the peacock shows no interest in her and then falls in love with her and vice versa. A heart-wrenching story because she goes away, comes back, has an ecstatic meeting with the peacock, who is then locked away with the other birds in the park and pines away and dies. In the story of the crow, too, there is a vulgar, vindictive man against a child (Small) and her protected beloved crow, a mischief-maker. Small is a lot like Jane Eyre as a child, a courageous rebel.

O dearest Monster August 25, '02
what sad & awful news that you have
to leave your beautiful HOUSE I, Mike,
am begging Net to find a sol- up from
so that you don't have to Fate in the
that plunge. So I'm sitting big
yoga posture weeping partly
unphilosophical tears,
Mum's fault because
she's too old
to love change and to be ready
for every- Thing. How could she forget
The Kings- bury blues - She can have the
blues anywhere, even in Paradise
though rumor has it that she's going to be cooling
her heels in Purgatory for a few millennia with
some of Dante's cats She committed venial
(the kind that aren't mortal, no? I wouldn't know)
sins enough to sink the Titanic for the 3rd
time — The second was in the movie
— Mum is slightly ga-ga today.
Eleanor interviewed the woman who wrote about
Sylvia Plath & Ted Hughes who did terrible
heart-breaking things that a cat like me
would never do - you know, jealousy, etc
has been mowing the lawn
was as long as Samson's hair.
Mum and I sympathize deeply
with you and
your mum in your PLIGHT

PS Could you bring me some old daisy
heads (still on stems there) to plant
the seeds HERE for next year?
NOT TOO DRY!! Not the roots, just heads

much love

I love you mum's Big Bird.

⌒

August 25

Oh dearest Mouser what sad & awful news that you have to leave your beautiful HOUSE. I, Mike, am begging Net to find a solution so that you don't have to take that plunge. So I'm sitting in the yoga posture weeping big unphilosophical tears, partly Mum's fault because she's too old to love change and to be ready for everything. How could she forget the Kingsbury blues. She can have the blues anywhere even in Paradise though rumor has it that she's going to be cooling her heels in Purgatory for a few millennia with some of Dante's cats—She committed venial (the kind that aren't mortal, no? I wouldn't know) sins enough to sink the Titanic for the 3rd time—the second was in the movie.

Mum is slightly ga-ga today. Eleanor interviewed the woman who wrote about Sylvia Plath & Ted Hughes who did terrible heart-breaking things that a cat like me would never do—you know, jealousy, etc. Sylvie has been mowing the lawn which was as long as Samson's hair. Mum and I sympathize deeply with you and your mum in your PLIGHT.

Much love

⌒

AUGUST 28. Another cloudless day. Dixie[60] called while I was brushing my teeth & talked about the picture of *Squeak*, his grief-filled eyes, my dream about Sarah in the sun, her trip with Anne Meigs to the little town in Connecticut near Guilford where lots of Meigses were born and died. She and Anne went to an old graveyard and saw the graves of *Silence and Submit* ... and their father Janess (?) (I never did hear this correctly) in 17-something. And I'd had trouble believing in the twins' existence—and this was such poignant proof.

SATURDAY, SEPTEMBER 7. Yesterday my BOSE radio came by UPS without any charge (yet). Suzanne unpacked it, read instructions, hooked it up. It's *beautiful*, finely made, easy to learn even by me, and the tone is wonderful.

⌒

September 7

Oh Mouser—everything seems to be topsy-turvy at Olivia Street. Marisa vient de téléphonêr rentrée de l'Ecosse and this morning your Mum's fax with that poor cat saying why have you put a clothes pin upside down on my

---

60. Mary's niece, daughter of Sarah.

nose? Loretta said that someone played with the photo & the clothes pin isn't there but the mere suggestion is hard on my cat-pride.

Your dear Mum is a model of calme. I'd be in a tizzy down there what with 102° and thunder and doves poor doves. Even I who am so heroic would hide my eyes & ears & whiskers and old Mum gets nervouser every minute, though it's only about 29° here & the AC is on & I haven't seen any doves. In fact I think the birds are poised to go South. How I miss the 2 crows and birds I never saw. Goodbye dear Mouser. I'm giving in to a state of non compos mentis with Mum.

Give much ❤ to your Mum

SEPTEMBER 8. Last night I was using the remote control quite close to the radio and a loud raspy noise came out and terrified me. Did it sound strange afterwards, some of the tones missing? The fear of having to send it back to be fixed, my beautiful BOSE. And my hearing-aid battery too made a kind of shriek this morning, followed by silence. This happens when the battery is dead? Bad omens. Last night Miky was lying close against my side, tail toward me. I stroked him along his back and felt a whole series of hard matted lumps, impossible to get off without cutting them. My heart sank. Yesterday Loretta and I called him together at 7:30. He was sitting at Gloria's with her grey cat and just looked without moving, then slowly got to his feet and started over. He had a terrible time getting over the fence. Later I suggested to L. that we think of a way of making it easier for him. Steps, she said, two boxes or bushel baskets or crates. The latter, I think. He still eats quite well, seems to prefer dry to canned food. Two pink roses—one on the very top of a 6 ft. high stem, the other lower. Hot again. 32° today.

Loretta just said that she saw Mike jump nimbly over the fence a few minutes ago. Also BOSE works well. My alarmism!

∾

September 14

Très cher Mouser—Enfin tu es témoin de ce paysage resplendissant, etc., après ton séjour dans la rue Olivia. Ta chère Mum était ici hier même avec moi MIKE autour de son cou. *(Mum seems to think I'm much rounder than I am.)*

Sylvie who is awfully nice to me is saying magic spells over the garden like the little collapsing four-leaf clover S. & L. gave us. Mum is digesting Karl Siegler's[61] *kind words about her unseen book, of all unexpected happenings. Plus the arrival of Marianne and her affectionate hugs at the end. Wonders will never cease as Mum's mother used to say. Personally I think Mum spends too much time chatting with ghosts, I'm sure they have better things to do like making friends among cats like Tidi and Pitty, even that highbrow Lily who felt superior to me, Miky. Oh dear, Mum hasn't called Diana yet. Just between you and me and your mum she, the dear old croak, suffers from the procrastinations of old age. Love to you & your dear mum.*

∾

61. Her editor and publisher at Talonbooks.

SEPT. 14,'02

Très cher Mouser – Enfin tu es témoin de ce paysage resplendissant, etc, après ton séjour dans la rue Olivia. Ta chère Mum était ici hier même avec moi MIKE autour de son con- (Mum seems to think I'm much rounder than I am) Sylvie who is nice to me, is magic spells garden like collapsing — is awfully saying over the The little four leaf clover Square us. Karl — Mum is digesting Ziegler's kind words about her unseen book, of all unexpected happenings. Plus the arrival of Marianne and her affectionate hugs at the end. Wonders will never cease as Mum's mother used to say. Personally I think Mum spends too much time chatting with ghosts, I'm sure they have better things to do like making friends among cats like Tidi and Pitty, even that highbrow Lily who felt superior to me. Miky. Oh dear, Mum hasn't called Diana yet. Just between you and me and your Mum she, the dear old crook, suffers from the procrastination of old age. Love to you & your dear Mum.

September 21

Très cher Mouser—I, Mike, was very glad to hear from you. Ici, hélas, Mum et moi ne voyons jamais la pleine lune. *She's not in the right place in our smog-filled sky and Mum goes to bed too early and discourages my moon walks. Tell your Mum my Mum is reading her elegant little new book*[62] *which is the cat's whiskers which is the highest praise a cat can give. Bellissima! And please thank her for the dédicace which makes her puff up her feathers like a ruffed grouse. I Miky am afraid this may go to her old head. By the way you must tell your Mum not to exaggerate Karl Siegler's words about the book. Of course he wants to see it. So Mum is sending him a copy and he's coming to say what he thinks Nov. 15th. So she prays you not to be over-optimistic as is your wont.* LOVE

---

62. *Ecrire: des rencontres humaines* (Montreal: Éditions Trois-Pistoles, 2002). Dedicated to "Mary Meigs, une grande artiste."

FROM: MARY MEIGS

Sept. 21, '62

Très cher
hear from
voyons
She's hot in
in our
goes to
discourages
Tell your Mum my mum
her elegant
book is the
which is the
cat's whiskers
which is the
highest praise a
cat can give. Bellissima!
her for the dédicace which makes her puff up
her feathers like a ruffled grouse
I Mikey am afraid this may go to
her old head. By the way you must
whomp   tell your Mum not to exaggerate
whomp   Karl Zeigher's words about
the book. Otherwise he wants to see it
So Mum is sending him a copy and he's coming to
say what the he thinks Nov. 15th. So she prays
you not to be over-optimistic as is your wont.
LOVE

Mouser, I, Mike - was very glad to
you - Oui, hélas, Mum et moi ne
jamais la pleine lune
the right place
smog-filled sky and Mum
bed too early and
my moon walks
is reading
little new
Milky is moon-struck

OCTOBER 4. Tomorrow, Saturday, M.C.'s birthday & I almost forgot. 63rd? She's in Trois Rivières at a poetry conference and reading. A long time seems to have gone by. I've been to the Montreal General to the ER for a night with lots of tests. Elizabeth came there sweetly for a day & brought bedpan. A small stroke. I feel as though various faculties dimmed—memory, reasoning power, hearing & sight were worse. Ears so blocked by wax that I could hardly hear at all. Dr. K. came and took some out, it was excruciating and made me cough so he decided to ask the nurse to wash it out with olive oil ... Meantime—the garden is there everyday with no frost.

The clematis still blooming, nasturtiums. Suzanne picked a last phlox blossom. Snapdragons? It's getting warmish & windy again. No leaves off. Happening tonight? (One of Cynthia's purple-blue pansies.) ...

The *Chicken* film was meant to make chickens seem lovable and intelligent—chickens as souls vs. the billion $ product for eating only. Since I was already convinced I was horrified by the industry and enchanted by the different chickens, specially the one at the end, a white silk hen dense with feathers who was like our Sarah in her passion for her chicks but gave up her life by protecting them from a hawk.

OCTOBER 8. Cold, sunny, blown pink-white roses still bright & straight high on their stem. Yesterday Sylvie picked the beautiful pink bud for M.C.'s birthday & she may take it Wednesday with her to Italy ... Today a huge tiredness and ineptness & failure to accomplish a single thing. Both M.C. & Claire have grippy colds. Miky doesn't feel well. Sleeps silently under my bed for hours & I think he's died ... This eternal summer greenness must upset the whole cycle of the trees and plants ...

OCTOBER 10. A warmish day. 4°–14°. The flowers in the house seem to be motionlessly holding the summer with their brightness—the nasturtiums, the flatness of their leaves like water lilies the one zinnia, bright red-orange, the green & white ground cover and then the rose, alone, in full perfect bloom now, still & magical. A symbol for M.C.? I couldn't give it to her. I didn't want to shock it, bruise it, make it wait for water, leave it alone while she goes to Italy. Its leaves are dark & glossy. It and the flowers are a fulcrum for the summer. A tiny red bud is opening.

124

October 11. Loretta about to come. The garden unchanged. A few nasturtiums peeping out from under the protective parasols of their leaves. Our rose is in full bloom, the flowers inside are almost unchanged, clematis outside still unchanged.

October 12, Saturday. Overslept, almost till 7. *A long dream about a young elephant in a wagon drawn by what I thought was a horse but turned out to be a dark hound-like dog with big, flat, square ears. At one point in this dream which I did my best to hang on to but shattered into pieces like the one the other night the dog was close up, looking intently at me & rather frightening.* At the same time Miky was trying to wake me up by walking over me. I tried to push him away but was tangled up in the covers. Elizabeth had to pull me up.

Very unsteady. I have the feeling that the stroke isn't quite over or hasn't quite begun. The CAT scan results haven't come back yet ...

October 13. A colorless day, the sun exerting a quiet pressure ... Another long dream last night that I couldn't retrieve before it shattered. *I meet Marie-Claire at the bottom of a big hill, a beautiful park. I have my black pocketbook with me but there's no money in it. M.C. helps me.* I think this is about boosting my morale; she's been doing this in a concentrated way lately—publicly praising me, dedicating the little book to me & assiduously coming to see me.

I'm not in a state when I can correctly interpret people's behavior—too paranoid—M. *seemed* to be sitting with her back turned to me & to talk the whole time to M.C. but M.C. was a little behind her on my bed and I was really glad not to try to talk ... It astonished me, though that M.C. ruffled her hair ... It showed something relaxed and intimate (in Mother's informal sense) between them that she didn't mind showing me. For we hide everything from each other for some reason. It seems to be a condition for our deep friendship.

A constant feeling of anxiety for someone or several at once, fear for friends with cancer, friends travelling, the terrorism that now permeates every single day everywhere. I remember that Sarah, not yet in our horrible world, looked with terror at the stones under her feet on the beach at Woods Hole, was miserable there the whole time for there was always something that threatened her safety, above all, her equilibrium.

October 19, Saturday. Dark & rainy & depressing. Cough still.

OCTOBER 21. Two dreams—only fragments left. *In the first I kiss the nose of a tiny brown goat, small & hard. In the second I'm lying facing a teenage Indian girl. Tenderness from each. Nice.*

The flutter of a big flock of starlings (short tails but grey) in the Dolgo.

Between this entry and the next, Mary suffered a collapse with stroke-like symptoms. The CLSC discovered an imbalance in her blood composition and she was sent to the Jewish General where she was treated for a week and a half. When she returned home she was in high spirits, and, as far as anyone around her could tell, was on the mend.

NOVEMBER 12.[63] Dream. *A train is coming into a station. But it isn't a train, it's a small old-fashioned carriage drawn by at least twelve pairs of coal-black horses that tread soberly and quietly ahead. There is no room for people in the carriage. We are at Woods Hole. They are people who have died, dressed in black, many more coming.* I cling to the image of the 12 pairs of black horses and little black carriage all night.

NOVEMBER 15.[64] Clearing—flame tree orange & yellow.

On the afternoon of November 15, Karl Siegler came for a two-hour visit to discuss possible publication of this book. Mary showed him the preface she'd written, the freewriting and the faxes. An hour after he left she fell and was taken to the hospital. She died two hours later of a cerebral hemorrhage.

63. Last entry in journal.
64. Noted in agenda.

Mary in her blue lift-assist chair with a friend's dog. Photo by Ann Pearson.

Freewriting

The following selections of Mary's freewriting are printed here exactly as they first appeared. These were five- or ten-minute exercises. If some of them seem brief for ten or even five minutes of nonstop writing, it's not because I've edited them down. Mary—anyone who knew her knew this about her—was not one to go on. Mary was dry, she was pithy, she was minimalist. In this respect her freewriting was like Mary herself. The cardinal rule of freewriting is you keep your pen moving. But sometimes in the middle of a freewrite I would look over and see that Mary's pen had stopped, indeed that she'd lifted it from the page. Looking up I would find her deep in thought, evidently contemplating her next line. I scolded her for cheating but it never made any difference. What issued from Mary's pen when it did contact the page was always so fresh and bracing that I finally stopped calling her on it at all.

Exact dates were missing for the first few samples but I've relied on Mary's notes and my own memory to place them more or less in the order of creation.

Above: Mary at her garden gate with Fallada, the horse's head gatepost.
Below: Mary's chair and table in the dining room, her last work space.

April, 2001

In song turns the daily. In the deaf ear turns the death of the daily a deafness of some listening spirit not an ear though the deaf ear doesn't help the deaf spirit is deaf to the fresh snow thrown like custard pies on the bare trees, to slapstick it hears the snide laugh and it hears the acuity or massive dark weight of blankness. Does the daily turn to song and epiphany? Yes, the little epiphany is laughter bubbling from no reality from necessity like a bird's song— hormones laughing hormones' song the healer the daily.

APRIL 2001

With your hand turning to stone. The literal atoms not an interesting stone more like cement the heavy listlessness and brute no less interesting than paralysis. Would that it were sandstone, the stuff of sunshine the mother of sand or vice versa. Warm stone not brimstone whatever the petrified interior of a cement mixer. I have become this.

The commonplace miracle. That so many miracles take place. I can't think straight about the everyday wonder of miracles: maybe *all* is miracle and anything commonplace is miraculously commonplace. It is an inside-out miracle when something miraculous is explained and becomes commonplace. Can you say that the sun going round the earth was miraculous. Nobody thought so. The movements of the spheres used to baffle and boggle my mind in the old days when miracles were more surprising but not more frequent. But I can't pursue this elusive point how can a miracle baffle when it is as obvious as the nose on your face. A troll could explain it, a fruit-fly could explain it. Look at me, she says.

APRIL, 2001

The blind and weeping bear. We can't speak of this image which is an exact description. Everybody weeps the python weeps the whale weeps on the beach the elephant, Sadie, lies down in the circus and sobs and is comforted. How rare it is that Sadie has been comforted. Well I'm getting distraught and hate my fellow-people like an old creaky phonograph—in the sweet-smelling hayfield. The Spanish were scared of mad cow disease and a cow came to protest against their intention to slaughter her. She was crying. She was in the *Montreal Gazette*. The Hindu saga in Almanabad says you have seven lives to go through and perhaps the next will be the cow.

We are not sure of sorrow. Which is one of the major sorrows like the major Tarot cards. Sorrow sometimes so simple for so simple a thing something that hasn't returned our love or has been very ambiguous about it. I remember the spider hanging on her thread over the dining-room table. She was too motionless too like a state of rigor mortis. They buried her with tears in a tiny part of the garden they grieved for years and keep her in their memory perhaps the truest love they have ever enjoyed. Perfect things with eight legs with superhuman eyes. The overlooked the unloved they are our polestars. That is all I have to say—the crux of the wonder of being alive.

MAY 15, 2001

Hope has grown grey hairs. Hope was old, poor thing, older than the five nuns. Does it mean that old grey-haired hope is less capable of hoping? Ageism again? Old grey-haired hope is perhaps *more* hopeful, hope is ingrained like the lines of her poor old face. She believes at last that the sky won't fall on her. Her name is Henny Penny. She is going to change it to Hope. Ms. Hope. Henny Penny is too intimate. Her hope muscles have been firmed up by constant exercise. The hope-abs. In the face of other people's flabbiness she flexes and smiles triumphantly. There is hope! The ship will not be dashed on the shore, the nuns will not drown. They will pick themselves up, shake themselves like a water spaniel or an osprey and skip hand in hand to the nearest nunnery. Gerard Manley Hopkins will never forgive them for being so happy. The Holy Martyrs would not have approved. The nuns will not be canonized. They must practice centuries of despair. And then the cameras will roll again.

May 29, 2001

In a dream I asked, "Did you call?" I waited, I said your name over and over, you didn't answer or open the door. Are they refusals for all time? Though when you were alive there was that sudden bright look of recognition once, a gathering of your living being in greeting. That much my subconscious is willing to grant. If only we could force the deadlock, a tiny motion and the sound of something falling into place. Like winning the lottery. But we have to die first.

They can't cook their own dinner. I have become one of them, the thought of cooking my own or other people's dinner makes me faint with false terror floods my adrenal gland with fears of living usefully again all the memories of stoves gas and electricity and wood and coal. Vistas of sea and Maine woods. The smooth round head and heart-melting dark eyes. The smooth putting of one foot in front of the other over mossy paths and rocks.

June 13, 2001

That winter it seemed the city. Was a wilderness of seeming without being. It, too, seemed in an effort to be being beyond seeming. A barrier of snow of course and days when it curved over walls and made icy glittering fringes bright as a sliver of sunshine.

Held you back. Have you ever turned on your shoulder? Even the thought impedes thought that holds me back and turning, the salvation of sleep is suspended on a lightly trembling anxiety the attempt to arrest thought and there is that mass of nothing again so densely heavy that it clogs every brain passage.

Looking for mushrooms. Something weightless and beautifully almost airborne united with that mushroom smell so earthily eloquent that it can never speak more truly of compost and transformation. Any earthworm could tell you that. Yes, tallying up my joys where can I find one that satisfies the senses with the psyche thrown in. The sublime delicacy ...

August 7, 2001

Shame is a rusty edge. Must I refuse the temptation to pick everything apart? Shame for me is not a rusty sharpness, not a dull clarity, is not the orange-brown jaggedness but formal edge of Sandy's iron star, the beautiful metamorphosis merging iron with light with humidity. It is closer to mold, to an abominable smell that can be recalled in the middle of the night, that suffuses the body with burning heat, mounts steadily to the crown of the head. I know about shame that it is more like poisonous burning gas than a rusty edge. It can outlive the life-span of plutonium. It will outlive memory. It can't be stepped on in a cow pasture. Lockjaw doesn't impress it. It enters the souls of animals.

October, 1, 2001

She who thinks deeply. She doesn't think deeply. Did she ever? She knows that deceptive certainty—that this is a deep thought that no one has ever thought before. It may be that a river will change course if you look at it long enough it may be that deep thoughts cannot be thought by someone who was born with a spoon in her mouth. This is the most corrosive deep thought that I ever thought. It has touched my grey matter with drought.

Votre avenir est là! Your future is there ... How comfortable and inhabitable these futures were—when? When we were comfortable in our mistakes—and there was room for optimism in even the smallest space—the airhole a fiddler crab makes in the sand. The small places where there's always room to meditate. Mussels meditate waiting for the next wave and the bracing smell of salt water. We must open ourselves to minute pleasures.

November 6, 2001

Away from Arid Stone. The thought of water lives in arid stone, when it was shaped by patient waves when it considered a new becoming. A patient though sometimes violent initiation into sex. Never say arid when talking to a stone you may be struck by an enraged stone. Don't be deceived by an arid heart which sometimes begs a stone to melt it, pouring the nutrient of sea-salt into its parched thirst. Stones are old life crone stones.

Black dog sprawled cool porcelain. Oh how I have loved a black dog sprawled and the porcelain sheen on its coat like a black Angus—all innocent pride and a dog's smiling satisfaction. How I will never cease mourning the archetypes dogs & cats their deep joy in themselves alive with love beating in their hearts—the grace of their sprawling. I ache for another glimpse of a porcelain paw and its leathery black toenails. My Emily, my Lily remember me beyond the grave.

January 22, 2002

Then I was back in it. To be sucked back in it even after heroic will-power and resistance. Like the secret wish to fall, the very slight movement to the left or the right or backward or forward. A chair, a toilet, are solid enough. A table can tip over with everything on— you'd be amazed by the strength of a falling body. But I can be back in something more than a state of equilibrium. I can be in a state of violent disequilibrium. When my mind is spinning like a wobbling gyroscope, or a drunken top. Or a nightmare.

FEBRUARY 14, 2002

Out of kindness comes redness. Particularly if you find someone else's kindness embarrassing. Or if someone else finds her kindness to you embarrassing. There are so many reasons for redness, unkindness is the most appropriate. My mind is clogged with unspent redness today of too much sleep or the storing up of frustrated dormant worker bees in my head waiting for some reason to unlock the signal of life.

February 22, 2002

Where the tongue is sent to penetrate. Full of promise and ambiguity you might say. Let us hope that it's welcome, this tongue that obeys an inexorable command. Did you send it and who are you to take such a liberty? My tongue can hardly articulate the letters of the alphabet without feeling it has had it with articulation of all kind. Baby elephants have to be taught to use those fine-tuned instruments, their little trunks, they need a mother to teach them.

The space where each of us finds our own body may be the size of a small unwelcoming bed or it may be somewhere we look hard and can't find our own or anybody else's body. Bodies are so hard to come by. I remember looking without success. Were these mine these unfamiliar limbs that said what should we do next? I didn't want to find a body that didn't know what to do next. It reminds me of the elephant who killed 3 of her babies before it occurred to her (after kicking it around for a while) that she wanted to be a real mother.

March 21, 2002

Encouragement meant nothing. How I've struggled to feel joy but lo and behold I'm in a joyless state. Warm encouragement strikes like a dead pancake. This is called a negative state; it is called ingratitude or tepid indifference. It's another form of hopelessness which is the eleventh deadly sin, for I know people who are saving the world. They have signed a peace pact with salmon, they have set them free.

Do not come down ... I'm living an incoherent day because I came down, obeyed gravity and hit my head. Now a thought trickles in like water giving life to dry clay. It is—"that bush over there is quite beautiful, it has been transformed by snow in less than half an hour. Once it was the flame tree, the vision that sang in October. Now it is a snow-blossoming March bush—& I croak my toad's song under its roots."

April 3, 2002

Now all my teachers are dead except silence. Silence won't be still like those others whom I beg to speak, extra sensory speech that the bees can understand and translate into movement, straight up or left or right. They will tell us in silent dance motion what the dead ones left unsaid. So much unsaid, there, of course, waiting for interpreters and a sunny day. It would be nice to learn another language, anything without sound. The sound of my voice sounds like a toneless platitude. If it were the silence of a butterfly's wings beating how profound with meaning it would be.

MAY 1, 2002

The shadow stayed where it was before. A poem speaking of doom of course. The shadow rolls forward and stays so spookily—that's the quiet of Armageddon. If I draw it tight around me I may begin to laugh. Negative laughter can be practiced, can be a healing force and too much light can kill. I will try never to eat a fish again or look into their eyes full of terror. Let the shadow stay.

June 11, 2002

A letter which can wither. Like a look or perhaps its contents have been a flower and fade, a pressed flower. My great aunt Anne's letters, kindly sharp and prickly. She was pressed to an extreme transparent fragility. She may have been an old-fashioned rose once, with a quite bristly moustache, with an almost soundless voice, with an anxious look between her black eyebrows and pinched nose. Such flowers are extinct now, they were not protected. She was pressed in a Bible.

Act so that there is no use in a center. Enough to have a circumference and the rest will take care of itself. Gertrude Stein made herself circular after much concentration; it was evidence of female power.

July 18, 2002

Sometimes it is inconceivable that I should be the age I am. What age am I? I am that critical age that corresponds with the age I am. It is an unwanted equilibrium when I will always be the age I am in horrid harmony with a phantom age that tries vainly to be younger in spirit at least and feel that effort as a reprimand. The age I am has become an imposition of a punishment—so many years for the equivalent offense. I would rather be a cicada singing my life's end.

SEPTEMBER 3, 2002

I lounged in a lounge chair waiting for the sun. Like my twin in the dream. The sunshine had come, it had a lingering look but there was no hint of a storm in it. She dreamed it for me, she said, to explain her silence. You could give me a few words, I said. The kind that make me laugh, a glad laugh. She said it's not really a laughing matter, we discover that when we can discuss it with Silence and Submit who hadn't yet learned to talk.

The fire of speech is killing her. She's lucky, I think—a good way to go and much better than dry ice which burns without eloquence. Poetry is the fire of speech. I'm saving a little bit from the *Oxford Book of 17th Century Verse* like "the fine rain down doth rain" or "mine eyes dazzle"—and the fire begins to kill me. That's how larks die, said a sage.

September 12, 2002

What exchange, your hands. This poet, mad with tenderness, doesn't know about Emily Carr's monkey Woo, her little hands as warm as ours, how they could tear hats to pieces or touch Emily's face in tender adoration. Our long ago ancestress. And now human beings like the taste of blood and hyenas like to listen to chamber music and lunatics advertise DNA's to live forever.

With both hands she takes my feet. This woman is obsessed by extremities. Perhaps she has never known the joy of being an amphibian. A whale makes love with neither hands nor feet; chooses, in fact, to love without them. But her baby has a marvellous sense of mother love when they touch.

And I said to my mother. Silently using my special speech for the dead. Now we can talk and answer each other like friends. Mother said with a smile, the trouble was we shouldn't have been talking. Now we understand each other without words. Being alive is an obstacle to friendship between mothers and children.

October 8, 2002

We don't know where they came from. We don't know how to track them. Their clues are invisible and do not reveal themselves. They used to answer my questions, now they make a strange answer inside my eardrums. My impression is that it's too late. A blurred whirring that I can't hear.

Waiting for another train to pass. In another direction. The feeling of being headed toward doom. The feeling of being scared, of being herded by an ignorant madman, of being helpless. But I don't want to go in this direction.

October 22, 2002

Now that we have learned to fly. There is no fear except the fear of forgetting. This happens all the time. For instance dancing, I could waltz in my head but my feet could not imagine the rhythm or direction. Where did this ignorance begin? It's a pervasive blank that seems to have crept into the cells of my brain and to wobble down to my feet. Things have made tracks—flying, dancing. They can be imagined. It's like the fake imagining I have when I see superior riders.

The following samples were written two days before Mary's death. I came over to visit, expecting to find her in bed. She'd just gotten back from the hospital and was not getting around very well. But as soon as I entered the house I heard her calling from the dining room—"Leeza?"—and walked in to see her sitting up and waiting for me at her very cluttered writing table. "Mary!" I said. "There you are!" "Here I am," she said, with that irony, that pithiness, that never deserted her. "Mary, do you think you're well enough to write today?" "Well my brain feels a little foggy, but I want to try," she said. And write we did.

November 13, 2002

I realize that this is an impure desire of mine. The question is what makes it impure. Is there an alchemy in each of us that works at refining desire or do dreams alter desires by changing their images? Last night I dreamt that twelve pairs of coal-black horses passed me, drawing a short carriage (black) along a railroad track.

Our history has a bumpy geography. We are reduced to translating time into landscape. But perhaps rocks are more eloquent than cries of pain. In a hospital sound speaks volumes but I would much rather be on a beach, a dictionary of pain. Today I found a polished grey pebble that said ouch.

Mary's garden at Grosvenor Avenue.

Afterword

Agitation on a Brick Wall

in memory of Mary Meigs

I

It is such a relief, she confesses when I visit her the first time after the stroke. It finally happened. Her face looks relaxed, different from the previous weeks when she was haunted by pre-stroke symptoms which she observed adamantly: high blood pressure, extreme pallor, shattered vision with fragmented patterns all of a sudden moving through the room.

She had been waiting for it, preparing for it, anxious and tense for weeks during that summer. How would the stroke hit her? As it had her mother and one of her brothers? From them she knew how a person looks after a left-brain stroke, how speech and language skills might be affected as well as the right hand, walking, balance. She was prepared for all of it, and she was lucky. Hers was a right-brain stroke that didn't touch the language center or her writing and drawing hand ...

II

She would be sitting at the far end of her dining room table when the helper of the day arrived at eleven o'clock in the morning, inevitably interrupting her writing hours—her precious alone time for which she fought ferociously after each of her numerous falls and the hip replacement surgery and the pacemaker surgery. At times we would all hover over her, driving her mad with worries about her next fall and even more with the threat to shrink her alone time, expanding the helpers' presence instead.

I heard her raise her voice only once: So what if I fall! she exclaimed. If I fall, I fall. Either I'll fall on a seat or on the floor. Either I'll break something or I won't. It is just there, worst-case scenarios included.

She fought for writing hours like a wild animal who has to go back into the cage for the rest of the day.

All day long now there would be somebody working in her rooms, crossing to and fro in front of her table, talking, maybe laughing loudly, singing loudly, turning the radio on, destroying the arrangement of her kitchen, removing items from places they had kept for decades and establishing an order of their own. She could do nothing but watch.

How is it? I asked once. It was very hard at the beginning, she said. I always thought I knew the perfect way of housekeeping and felt the urge to teach everybody. She looked at me. I got used to it, she said. After all, I depend on helpers now.

My mind is seeping out, she said. I dream of prisons and confinement. I am confined, that's a fact.

The helpers walked in the door, each one of us, always hoping that everything would be fine, that Mary would sit near the window and write. And there she was. She was always there. She had to be there. This was her bitter pill, to be confined to the house, to observe her mobility shrink to smaller and smaller loops, even indoors.

Not to go out anymore to concerts, art shows, book launches, to the movies. Not to drive. And shopping. How I miss shopping! she said. And birds. She always wanted to know what birds there were, when I came back from a trip to the country. Mary, I saw a cardinal, I would say. A cardinal! she would exclaim, clutching her heart. Doesn't it have the loveliest song in the whole world!

What other birds were there? She fixed me with her eyes, and I squirmed, trapped between unfamiliar French and English names for birds and a scarce bird-knowledge to begin with.

Cut off from her studio in the country from one day to the next, from whole summers in the country. Cut off from her luminous writing office upstairs in her Westmount home too, and from her small drawing room. The inspiration is in the upstairs rooms, she said.

She lived downstairs now, in the semi-light behind milky curtains ...

During the last year of her life, she was in the company of artists and friends who would stay with her eight hours a day. Intense ephemeral states of co-habitation. The helpers were witnesses to her changing states of being, high-soaring moments and what she called her collapsed state of mind. Since she could not go out anymore, the world and cultural life had to come to her house. Colleagues, friends, writers, artists, editors, with their buzzing lives and busy daybooks, kept streaming in, all of them with little time, though some of them would stay beyond Mary's point of exhaustion.

We are not used to somebody staying at home all the time. To find a friend at the same place at every hour of the day, day after day, month after month, even in July and August. To be guaranteed that she will be there whenever we show up at the doorstep. It is a feeling we may know from our childhood if there was a mother, a father or a grandparent who stayed home. Other than that, it is an odd thing that is related to temporary or chronic illness, or to very old age ...

III

"Illness is the night-side of life, a more onerous citizenship," writes Susan Sontag at the beginning of her essay "Illness as Metaphor," and she continues: "Everyone who is born holds dual citizenship, in the kingdom of the well and in the kingdom of the sick. Although we all prefer to use only the good passport, sooner or later each of us is obliged, at least for a spell, to identify ourselves as citizens of that other place."

Mary adds another aspect to the image: "In old age we are forced to speak another language," she has written in her last notebook. "We are people who are forbidden to speak our mother tongue. The process of deterioration is made easy for us by memory loss, the accidental breaking of bones, the dimming eyes; each body selects its own way of inflicting damage willy-nilly ... "

The mother tongue of color remained the salient one in her life. Whenever I came to visit her in yet another hospital room I found depressingly ugly, she would make a comment on the play of light and shadow on a wall outside the window, sunlight that hit a tin decoration on a roof, the hourly changes in the leaves of a tree, the setup of a therapy room. "The whole place a visual joy," she writes. "Yesterday saw something purple and yellow juxtaposed."

There was a brick wall behind the neighbor's garden at Grosvenor Avenue that served her as a screen until the end of her life. "The shadows of branches and a few blowing maple leaves on the brick wall today," says one of her notebook entries, or "Agitation of shadows on the wall—a squirrel has run along a thin branch." Those sentences are scattered on the pages of her notebooks like the small agitations she caught from the angle of her eye behind the window where she would write. She perceived life entirely with a painter's eye, and being an avid searcher for colour and shape she found them everywhere.

—Verena Stefan

List of Caretakers
(in order of appearance)[65]

Leonie Reboldera, "L.," night nurse
Elizabeth Davidson, "Eliz.," or "E.," night nurse

Women associated with the community of Sugarloaf Key
Claudia Kuntze, "C.," Sugarloaf Key
Sandy Hagan, "S.," Sugarloaf Key
Barbara Vogel, "Vogel," Key West, FL
Kat O'Donoline, "K.," Huntsville, AL
Sally Willowbee, South Jersey, Sugarloaf Key
Alma Arauz, Sugarloaf Key

Montreal caretakers
Verena Stefan, "V.," (also came regularly for physical therapy)
Suzanne Boisvert, "S."
Sylvie Ste. Marie, "S."
Claire St. Aubin
Loretta Tarpin

65. Note: the fact that three of these women are abbreviated "S." means that the reader can't always be entirely sure who's being referred to. In most cases, though, it's clear enough from the context.

Sources for Freewriting Prompts
(incomplete list)

Bishop, Elizabeth. *The Complete Poems 1927–1979*. NY: Farrar, Straus and Giroux, 1969.

Carson, Anne. *Men in the Off Hours*. NY: Vintage Books, 2001.

Cixous, Hélène. *The Book of Promethea*, trans. and with an intro. by Betsy Wing. Lincoln: University of Nebraska Press: 1991.

Follett, Beth. *Tell it Slant*. Toronto: Coach House Books, 2001.

Freeman, Jan. *Hyena*. Cleveland, OH: Cleveland State University Poetry Center, 1993.

Hopkins, Gerard Manley. *A Hopkins Reader*, ed. John Picky. NY: Doubleday, 1966.

Marchessault, Jovette. *Triptych Lesbien*. Montreal: La Pleine Lune, 1980.

Merwin, W.S. *The Lice*. NY: Atheneum, 1979.

Namjoshi, Suniti. *Goja*. N. Melbourne: Spinifex Press, 2000.

Sitwell, Elizabeth. "Still Falls the Rain" (from unknown edition).

Stein, Gertrude. *Tender Buttons*. Los Angeles: Sun and Moon Press, n.d.

Swinburne, Algernon Charles. "The Garden of Proserpine" (from unknown edition).

Szymborska, Wislawa. *Poems New and Collected 1957–97*, trans. Stanislaw Barancak and Clare Cavanagh. Harvest Book, 1998.

ALSO BY MARY MEIGS

The Box Closet
ISBN 0-88922-253-3

In the Company of Strangers
ISBN 0-88922-294-0

Lily Briscoe: A Self-Portrait
ISBN 0-88922-195-2

The Medusa Head
ISBN 0-88922-210-X

The Time Being
ISBN 0-88922-374-2

Available from Talonbooks
www.talonbooks.com